The Movie at the End of the World:

Collected Poems

Other books by Thomas McGrath

Poems:

First Manifesto
The Dialectics of Love
    (in *Three Young Poets*, ed. by Alan Swallow)
To Walk a Crooked Mile
Longshot O'Leary's Garland of Practical Poesie
Witness to the Times!
Figures of the Double World
Letter to an Imaginary Friend
New and Selected Poems
Letter to an Imaginary Friend, Parts I & II

Novel:

The Gates of Ivory, The Gates of Horn

Children's Books:

Clouds
The Beautiful Things

The Movie at the
End of the World:

Collected Poems

Thomas McGrath

THE SWALLOW PRESS INC.
CHICAGO

Published by
The Swallow Press Incorporated
1139 South Wabash Avenue
Chicago, Illinois 60605

ISBN (cloth) 0–8040–0605–9
ISBN (paper) 0–8040–0606–9
Library of Congress Catalog No. 72–91918

This book is printed on 100% recycled paper

Most of these poems have appeared in magazines, and antholo-
gies, and thanks are extended to the editors of the following for
permission to reprint poems in this book: *Accent, Aegis, Ameri-*
can Dialog, Cafe Solo, California Quarterly, Carleton Miscellany,
Choice, Coastlines, Common Sense, Contemporary Reader, Crazy
Horse, Crescendo, Cross Section, Dacotah Territory, Democratia,
Denver Quarterly, Discovery, Far Point, Inferno, Interim, Lamp
in the Spine, Les Lettres Francaises, Limbo, Masses & Main-
stream, Meanjin, Measure, Modern Verse, Mojo Novigator (e),
Nation, New Anvil, New Mexico Quarterly, New Orleans Poetry
Journal, New Poets of England and America, Nomad, The Only
Journal of the Tibetan Kite Society, Our Time, Panama Red,
Poetry (Chicago), *Poetry Broadsheet, Poetry Los Angeles, Quet-*
zel, Refugee Journal, San Francisco Review, Scapecraeft, Signets,
The Sixties, Statement, Three Young Poets, Tri-Quarterly, Voices,
Voice of Scotland, Western Review, Where is Vietnam?, Win.

Fire, flood and the general attritions of time have complicated a
primitive system of record-keeping. If there are errors and omis-
sions I pray the editors of any magazines I have forgotten forgive
them.

for Genya and Tomasito

First the pork chops,
then morality.
—Brecht

I see the starres at bloudie warres
In the wounded welkin weeping.
—Anon.

A Note on the Book

This book gathers together most of the short poems I want to save. HOWEVER IT DOES NOT contain work from my main project of recent years, the long poem *Letter to an Imaginary Friend*, except for two short sections which appeared to me first as autonomous pieces, were published separately and had a life of their own.

Readers familiar with the poems here will find some changes of words and lines. These are not changes of substance but restorations of corrupted texts. One of the books from which I have taken some of the poems here was put together by a friend, in my absence, from unrevised and foul copy. Two or three were printed at times when I was out of the country and unable to read proof. In one case even the title of a book contained an error—*Figures From a Double World* should have been *Figures of the Double World*, the emphasis on the dialectic, on process, on states of the world rather than states of mind. In another case a poem for which I have a high regard has been yoked to a first line made incomprehensible by the addition of an *r* to the third word. Etc.

In the last section in this book, the New Poems, which is here considerably expanded, rather than splicing the new work on to the section as it stood in *New and Selected Poems*, I have interpolated the new and rearranged the old, in search of the order which any group of poems wants.

Contents

III: from FIGURES OF THE DOUBLE WORLD

IV: NEW POEMS

I: from
FIRST MANIFESTO
and
THE DIALECTICS OF LOVE

Get Out of Town

Get out of town before it's too late
While the speed boat is frozen in the arctic lake
While the cops are snoring in the frost-hung parlor
And the shotgun hidden under crumpled pillows.

Get out of town, cross the winter mountain.
There are arteries hardening. The mob yells murder,
But be stayed no one, yourself no traitor—
They will not be saved, themselves not try to.

Get out of town while the going is good.
Say the hard word. Kiss the girls goodby.
Let the boys wait forever in the gloomy barrens
A thousand miles from water and as far from wood.

Europe at Midnight — Newsreport

this moment is at war with all of time
with the slow climbing moon whose drifting hours
fall earthward softly as the petals fall
from some moonbending flower

and we like moths upon a point of time
make quaint conceits that all will be forever:
hearing the startled chimes: the steady work of the river:
dull knives of grass—wish if moths to be safely under glass

so to forget the insane noise of the clock
mockingly chuckling its two prayers in the gloom—
the idiot fates play with our lives in an empty room
and the heart beats sharp like the late machine-guns in the park

—Turn up the radio. Give us a tune.

and save this single moment in the dark hour of doom

Sentiments for a Valediction

Now when hand of lavish summer spends
In careless flowers lost coinage of the sun,
We, remembering our losses, stand
Cold in the sunlight, wishing summer gone,
And wish for another time and another land.

Sickening in furnished rooms, watch the soldier
Hands of clock march; think how callous years
Have made us never wiser but certainly, surely older;
Would turn from dirty dishes, push back chairs
And leave our half burnt cigarettes to smoulder.

Would mark the map: put X on any spot
Unknown to us. Go by the hidden lane
Soon from the city, hike it or if not
Take ship for somewhere, or take fastest plane,
Take bus for farthest frontier known of night.

Say so-long to dead ways walked before—
Leave clothes in closets, leaving sentry clocks,
Put on new faces, forgetting to lock doors
Or switch off lights, hoping to leave old aches
And emptiness behind, steer by the stars

Toward other darknesses. Far: and not in Fall
Return, but go and go beyond any Asia,
Leave no address, footprint nor public scrawl
"Wish you were here." There, learn some better ways,
New names for sun and summer, our own names last of all.

4

Up the Dark Valley

After the lean road looping the narrow river,
At a break in the valley, turned northward up the coulee,
Past the slow shallows where minnows, a tin flash
Patterned the trellised shadow. Then, leaving behind the last trees,
The spider sun laid on the hot face a tight miraculous web.

Northward then. All afternoon beneath my feet the ground gave
Uneven going. The colorless silence, unraveled by the flies,
Stitched again by the locusts, was heard, was smelled—
Swamp-smell, dead coulee water.

                                    And the easy hills,
Burnt brown, green, grass color, went on through the afternoon,
Then blue-gray in the blue shadow. The path went on.
Darkness hid in the draws. I was soon surrounded.
Only the wind sound now. All through the evening,
Homeward I walk, hearing no human sound.

The birds of darkness sang back every call.

A Way You'll Never Be

when you knock at the door and nobody comes
and you must go home to an empty room
and you walk up and down in a sick despair
or you call a number and there's no one there

when you're all alone in that nightly grave
and there's half a reason in the world to live
and there's not the ghost of a step on the stair
and the phone's taken out or they've cut the wire

5

then turn up the radio find if you will
how the good are happy in a gilded world
or go to the movies if you've got a dime
and learn to be happy on money and time

when the bridges are bombed and the rivers too high
and a nameless fear has wings in the sky
and the personal wireless is blocked by static
arrange your bones in a surrealist attic

or postpone forever what you're wanting now
and pray that all will be right somehow
not lost like gulls above an arctic sea—

O surely it's a way you'll never be.

Götterdämmerung

Trapped by the metaphysical gin
The innocent whores hang in the tree.
Enter death's lover, their love, axe-man:
Sweetly the heads fall one two three.

Sanctus. Them shall the fangèd music
Cover as over the crab the barking
Hyena seas. Whom death hath blinded
So light is a wild Egyptian dark.

Percival, Sluggsy, the Moll and the Gang,
With Grandpa Freud in their narrow beds,
Have pulled an ice-age over their heads
Or gun in their teeth have gone out bang bang.

Nightmare

This night water. A girl on the beach.
A speed boat yammers going nowhere fast.

In a similar situation, minus the speedboat, Whitman
Found similitude spanning all: stars, moons,
The usual catalogue. All enclosed in a circle—
It, perhaps, tightening like that of the Whatsit bird
Who flies a decreasing circle at increasing speed—
Finally flies through his bottom and disappears.

You could think great thoughts like this, perhaps, if you
Were a great poet, if you weren't quite so hungry.

Whitman's woman, of course, was somewhat older.
And it was by the ocean, not a lake, in a different country,
And besides the wench is dead.

Woodcut

It is autumn but early. No crow cries from the dry woods.
The house droops like an eyelid over the leprous hill.
In the bald barnyard one horse, a collection of angles
Cuts at the flies with a spectral tail. A blind man's
Sentence, the road goes on. Lifts as the slope lifts it.

Comes now one who has been conquered
By all he sees. And asks what—would have what—
Poor fool, frail, this man, mistake, my hero?

More than the hands on the lines and the back aching,
The daily wrestle with the angel in the south forty,
More than this forever lonely round

7

Round hunger and impotence, the prickly pair:
Banker or broker can have dreamed no fate
More bankrupt than this godlike heresy
Which asks of love more leave than extended credit,
Needs comradeship more than a psalm or surely these
Worn acres even if over them
Those trained to it see signs of they say God.

Portrait

At midnight in Brahms he murdered the radio,
Sent postman on false spoor to freeze in the barrens.
Handcuffed the doorbell, strangled the phone
Lived in a glass house and slept alone.

But the Mummy spun madly, its ticker tape trapped him—
"Who's sorry now?" chimed the clock in his guts.
The Roman candle in his skull was ablaze
And blew out - Jesus! - his bland glass eyes.

Jig Tune: Not for Love

Where are you going? asked Manny the Mayor.
What are you doing? asked President Jane.
I'll bet you're a bastard, said Daniel the Deacon;
We'll put you away where you'll never be seen.

There won't be no pardon, said Manny the Murderer.
There won't be no stay, said Tommygun Jane.
Said Daniel McBedlam, You won't go no farther;
My father won't even declare you insane.

For a Madman's Way, intoned Manny the Magnate.
The Public Good, shouted Editor Jane.
I think he's a Commie, cried Danny O'Garrote;
If he won't do murder, I call it a crime.

It's not a long drop, sang Manny the Hangman.
The rope will stop you, crooned Juryman Jane.
In a box long and black, chanted Danny Le Flack,
We'll suit you warm to keep out the rain.

All flesh is grass, sighed Manny the Mourner.
The handsome young man, wept Sob-sister Jane.
R.I.P., prayed Capital Daniel;
If he were alive we could kill him again.

You Can't Go Home

When the homing heart is coming round the mountain,
What would hope have there at the road's end?
The octave of trees ring out a bell of birds?
The long-haired scarecrow shakes a leg in schottische?

You would have, Sirs, what simple is and easy:
Classic meeting of heroes under the ample oaks:
The gifts exchanged, to one the blue ox, to the other that
    charmed shield
Inscribed: in peace the dragon-haunted sea
Whose green necks nibble on the shores of sleep.

From each his gift. To each the equal hand.
Then to that hearth where wintered warm was Love,
A flame-lipped Brunhild burning for your kiss.

But the sheep's in the meadows, the cow's in the corn.
There's been some changes made since you been gone.

Then rage outrageous as your outraged heart,
Your own, unique, your never equalled loss
Conjures up curses. And in your loss feel pride:
Your suffering is a fine patrician thing!
No one has ever—poor plebeian souls!—
Searched for the note, looked in the hollow tree,
Looked for the red stones hidden by the well-side,
Looked, are looking, finding the spring turns up
No forwarding addresses. No, no, no—

Then hail and farewell, Friends, Brothers, all away,
Lost as birds are on the mapless night of Asia,
As bells in wind beyond the stormy Hebrides—
And love O is lying under marble trees.

To Walk a Crooked Mile

1.

Lie on the bridge of midnight, top-most turn
And circle of the turning year. O Beloved, hear
The tempestuous fugue: its truckling trumpets: time's
New Year amphibian on the moment's stair—
    Sister Anne, Sister Anne
    That man's here again

Then climb jazz ladders to a midnight stark
As rigor mortis, where reptilian eyes
Look—as for lover?—is it the man with the knife
Ghosting the fungus reaches of the dark?

10

—But still see time as double featured in
The kiss and cuddle of the fractured show—
One face is always and as million as
The People's Army moving in the snow.

—Coming for Bluebeard? Surely coming—coming—
But can classic violence even save the head -
Less history? The heads perhaps will go a-roaming
Hurry, hurry for the pastures of the dead:

    Newsreel: the midnight harbors burn:
    The fleece of darkness curries the blown cabs:
    Fire is shaking like a housemaid's broom
    The stallion-simple towers. The candied curbs
    Are fenced with eyes, with the sick eyes looking:
        The Man with the Face, time's other face, the Moll.
        Grandpa and Egbert, Sluggsy and Percival
    Going to the fire.
                Looking for death. For death?
    Their Death? Death of our fathers. Yea
    Pax vobiscum
             who hath razed these towers

2.

Midnight is morning in the arms of love—
This love which has the strength to keep
Warm on one side only, yet may speak
The ordered syllables for even who
In all the islands of the night have found
Only the treachery of jungle peace;

Gives force and faith, and in the streets of death
Bears bread of witness like a secret oath:
Plenum of competence, range-finder, gives

11

Compasses to walk a crooked mile:
Can wait the phoenix hour, the ascendant sun—

See: from this bridge no midnight murders dawn.

The Topography of History

All cities are open in the hot season.
Northward or southward the summer gives out
Few telephone numbers but no one in our house sleeps.

Southward that river carries its flood
The dying winter, the spring's nostalgia:
Wisconsin's dead grass beached at Baton Rouge.
Carries the vegetable loves of the young blonde
Going for water by the dikes of Winnetka or Louisville,
Carries its obscure music and its strange humour,
Its own disturbing life, its peculiar ideas of movement.
Two thousand miles, moving from the secret north
It crowds the country apart: at last reaching
The lynch-dreaming, the demon-haunted, the murderous virgin South
Makes its own bargains and says change in its own fashion.
And where the Gulf choirs out its blue hosannas
Carries the drowned men's bones and its buried life:
It is an enormous bell, rung through the country's midnight.

❋   ❋   ❋

Beyond the corrosive ironies of prairies,
Midnight savannas, open vowels of the flat country,
The moonstruck waters of the Kansas bays
Where the Dakotas bell and nuzzle at the north coast,
The nay-saying desolation where the mind is lost
In the mean acres and the wind comes down for a thousand miles
Smelling of the stars' high pastures, and speaking a strange language—

12

There is the direct action of mountains, a revolution,
A revelation in stone, the solid decrees of past history,
A soviet of language not yet cooled nor understood clearly:
The voices from underground, the granite vocables.
There shall that voice crying for justice be heard,
But the local colorist, broken on cliffs of laughter,
At the late dew point of pity collect only the irony of serene stars.

* * *

Here all questions are mooted. All battles joined.
        No one in our house sleeps.
And the Idealist hunting in the high latitudes of unreason,
By mummy rivers, on the open minds of curst lakes
Mirrors his permanent address; yet suffers from visions
Of spring break-up, the open river of history.
On this the Dreamer sweats in his sound-proof tower:
All towns are taken in the hot season.

How shall that Sentimentalist love the Mississippi?
His love is a trick of mirrors, his spit's abstraction,
Whose blood and guts are filing system for
A single index of the head or heart's statistics.
Living in one time, he shall have no history.
How shall he love change who lives in a static world?
His love is lost tomorrow between Memphis and
        the narrows of Vicksburg.

But kissed unconscious between Medicine Bow and Tombstone
He shall love at the precipice brink who would love these mountains.
Whom this land loves shall be a holy wanderer,
The eyes burned slick with distances between
Kennebunkport and Denver, minted of transience.
For him shall that river run in circles and
The Tetons seismically skipping to their ancient compelling music

13

Send embassies of young sierras to nibble from his hand.
His leaves familiar with the constant wind,
Give, then, the soils and waters to command.
Latitudinal desires scatter his seed,
And in political climates sprout new freedom.
But curst is the water-wingless foreigner from Boston,
Stumping the country as others no better have done,
Frightened of earthquake, aware of the rising waters,
Calling out "O Love, Love," but finding none.

The Drowned Man: Death between Two Rivers

1.

Someone moves through the jungle
Where the East Side rears its neo-Tammany escarpment
Over East River toward the city of the dead, toward
    Brooklyn;
Past the opulent stinks, the sinks and pits of corruption,
Where canned heat dreams are pregnant with rancid
    dragons—
Immaculate conceptions!—

Someone, someone is moving:
The feet go eastward, past the callow pimps
Pasted on door-ways and past the wise, new-minted
Eyes of the semi-virgins. Waters of Israel
Open in paths before him: the Leaning Man,
Comes out of Egypt.

By the waters of his captivity,
He leans on the river rail. The enchanted liner,
A breathing bird upon the water's breast,
Beats for the windy capes, the secret cities

Of the lush South. The river stinks. Behind him,
The towers of Babylon—

Altar of profane love,
Each marvelous marble phallus. On the walls
The handwriting winks in easy translations of neon.
Over him the bridge no one has written an ode to,
And northward the monstrous Tri-borough, seeking
    direction
Puts out its feelers:

A symbol of indecision
For the Leaning Man, the semi-vertical man,
Man by a river, looking to westward, knowing
The terrible land wherein the Lost Tribes dwell,
And, hatches closed against night, the known world
Slowly submerging.

He assumes vertical stature
Standing, as the deck lists under the lip of water
He looks toward the city, inventing impossible justice:
Recalls other cries, and decision matures, remembering
Metal of headlines masked as life preservers:
Dives from the railing.

The East River upbore him:
Two-thirds submerged in the riptides under the bridgeheads,
In a montage of oil-smear, rotten fruit and wreckage—
Christ! his poor face split like a seed-pod sowing
In the crucified night an improbable human anguish—
The face of my brother!

2.

Full fathom five the East Side lies;
The West Side lies five fathom under.
A slow sea-change in the drowned veins,

15

The unfortunate human condition creates its pitiful
   wonders:
Unlikely fear has deepened into gills
And cynic's scales—armor against laughter;
The dearest nightmare is the dream of waking,
Waking to choke in the drowsy midnight waters:
The drowned eye builds in token its cheap ambiguous
   altars
In the Java Deeps of the Leaning Men, where the drunken
   small boat founders.

The little yachts of extended credit
Are lost where the naked rocks are lying
But the mighty slave-galleys of surplus value
Move on these human deeps, majestic, the black flag
   flying.
At dawn in Wall Street the gentle fishers
Dapple with nets the sunshot sound,
And all but the strangest swimmers are taken:
Between two rivers where my brother drowned—
In the waters of Manhattan, where he last went down,
Where the mad boy catches at his sunken moons and
   darkens the night with crying.

                    ❁   ❁   ❁

I heard them crying halfway up Delancy—
Poverty halleluiahs, neither private nor fancy.
      Tell me, Stranger, who was lost,
      Father, son or wholly ghost?

3.

No one has seen in the leaves, in the dark, crowding,
The immaculate mutinous bodies, or, shyly, the brutal
Inhuman faces of angels. Only of birds,
In the empty dark, the shameless voices puzzling

16

Some last year's song. The news is bad. Angels
Are scarce this year. A ghost perhaps? But no one
No one walking on a windward water. No one.

Darkness over the waters. The tame tides
Set to the impersonal moon which over Brooklyn
Scatters its loose money. The East River
Constant, turns to the inconstant sea,
A cortege of tired cigars, old photographs,
Letters of credit with their mouths sewn shut, newspapers,
Paler than funeral flowers, its dead men's bones
(All abstract emblems of our civilization)
Bearing my brother:

The tides set toward the Jersey coast, push southward,
Slack from wreck-wreathed Hatteras. And where
The Gulf Stream washes toward the glittering North,
The mystic fog-hung latitudes of myth,
Do those bones live?
                    Or in the under sea
Processional of equatorial drift,
Or swept beyond Lands End, tossed in the wind,
Or in the mile-long funnels of the dreaming interior
Made part of the steaming legend-haunted sea?

                    * * *

Someone is dying, someone is being born:
Out of the salt blood, fiercer than the sea
Where the human tide makes in the evening rush:
Grand Central-Times Square undertow,
Setting to a black moon over Harlem:
Something is dying. Something is being born.

There are ghosts among us. Who was that
In the tombstone hat, the meek hick jacket?
Out of a deeper drowning than the sea,

17

Out of the cynic north, in that season, the second, where
    all illusion is lost,
The obscure, terrible coming of our holy ghost.
I did not recognize him under the bridge:
Saw only our human weakness as denominator in that
    fraction.
But later, I remembered in the flat-lands hearing
That mountain speech, and in the mountains hearing
His speech as of cities, and in the cities hearing
His silence of hawks. And it was easy then
To think how tides had shortened the tough Rockies,
Washed out the Kansas Coast or in the river haunted
Landscapes of New England bore with them this specter
Which haunts all countries in the fifth season.
                                            And felt,
Ambiguous as hope but stronger, something crowding
The hollow channels of the blood, or swept between
The red islands, speaking with the timid tongue,
Naming the devils at the several compass points,
With words for the nightmares of our sunken world,
Calling insurrection, knocking at the tame heart—
"Sleeper awake."

                    * * *

The ambulance siren drifts in the blue night air.
With tentative provocation the first stars
Put out thin stalks of light, placing their formal
Decorations on a sleeping child. Somewhere
A nightmare sharpens and a man cries out. The young
Mother feels the child kick in her belly.
Once. Twice. And deeper than pain she feels
How out of the submerged life, the human winter,
The young god comes to whom all eyes shall turn.
One class dies. Another is being born.
Word becomes flesh. The Specter becomes real.

Someone is born with the bright face of your brother.

18

Many in the Darkness
November 1941

We sat in the park, but there was a war between us,
A dead moon over us and all around us
The shy and secret whisperings as of the tiny
Woods animals which in the high forest gather
Wind-fallen goods before the frost comes.

We praised as lucky all whose sure existence
(As of the careless moon, the dutiless squirrels)
Is not responsible for human history—
Feeling how our happiness, how hope must mount
Machine guns which other men yet have the firing of,
How liberty is seen in the form of a fighter plane
Millions look up at asking, Is it ours?

Our despair was temporary but not less painful.
Over us the moon was quiet about its business,
Pouring its constant light upon the naked beaches.
The squirrels built up their small defenses
Obliged to the fulfillment of a natural process.
Their leaf-lined cell, the brilliance of the moon,
The winter cannot touch and no touch tarnish.

The Dialectics of Love

1.

Under barley leaf and clover,
Lying cold, the faithless lover
Learns at last an amity
Which allows conformity.
Rocks and tree roots cabin him?

19

They will teach him discipline.
The rich and heavy turf above,
Closer press than any lover.
Virginal mortality
Closer than himself shall lie,
And all the weathers of his body bear
The frozen rigor of the winding year.

2.

Between brother Dexter and cousin Sinister
Frontiers are open toward the human winter,
And civil war in every sector
Murders, fidelity's frail perspective;
In the lover's counties, the hunting heart
Is haggard wherever desires start—
In his own nets is that bright hawk taken,
A willing captive, the old ties broken.
And fearful lovers all complain
The strict modality of change;
Feeling in all their ordered parts
The rebel soviets rising up,
They cry, "I am not; be not false"—
When each day finds them someone else:
Whom every hour creates anew—
He must seem false who would be true.

3.

What love the year shows to the spring
By autumn grows another thing.
And yet each season has its part
In the weathers of that impersonal heart:
The summer bourgeois revolution
Offers morality's pale solution—
Over the public eye and lip

The seal of personal ownership;
Prepares the realm for civil war
When right hand and left divided are
And the split heart cannot love the more
Public virgin or private whore.
Out of these warring opposites
Arises the needed synthesis:
At nodal points the personal love
Changes, if it is pure enough,
From single idol in man or woman
To equal love for all that's human.
And even in death the faithful lover
Under barley leaf or clover
His mating body still must share
With the transience of the winding year.

II: from
TO WALK A CROOKED MILE,
LONGSHOT O'LEARY'S GARLAND
OF PRACTICAL POESIE
and
WITNESS TO THE TIMES

The Seekers
Pueblo, Colorado 1940

Our grandfathers were strangers and their absurd notions
Said uncle to a century that built few fences;
Pragmatists, with six-guns, their dreams were never fancy;
Beyond their mustaches, their eyes eloped with nations.
Their caravans set wagon tongues at a peculiar star;
Led at last to mountains, they sought to map Fidelity—
Went loco in windy canyons, but, lost, they looked
       harder and harder.

Our fathers, more complex and less heroic,
Were haunted by more ghosts than an empty house.
Their joy was to thumb their hearts over. Masked like Freud
They entered their unconscious by the second story.
But what they were seeking, or how it looked or sounded,
We heard about only once in a blue moon,
Though they expected to know it if they ever found it.

Every direction has its attendant devil,
And their safaris weren't conducted on the bosses' time,
For what they were hunting is certainly never tame
And, for the poor, is usually illegal.
Maybe with maps made going would be faster,
But the maps made for tourists in their private cars
Have no names for brotherhood or justice, and in any case
We'll have to walk because we're going farther.

Deep South
Baton Rouge, 1940

These are savannas bluer than your dreams
Where other loves are fashioned to older music,
And the romantic in his light boat
Puts out among flamingos and water moccasins
Looking for the river that went by last year.

Even the angels wear confederate uniforms;
And when the magnolia blooms and the honeysuckle,
Golden lovers, brighter than the moon,
Read Catullus in the flaring light
Of the burning Negro in the open eye of midnight.

And the Traveller, moving in the hot swamps,
Where every human sympathy sends up the temperature,
Comes of a sudden on the hidden glacier,
Whose motives are blonder than Hitler's choir boys.

Here is the ambiguous tenderness of 'gators
Trumpeting their loves along a hundred miles
Of rivers writhing under trees like myths—
And human existence pursues the last,
The simple and desperate life of the senses.
Since love survives only as ironic legend—
Response to situations no longer present—
Men lacking dignity are seized by pride,
Which is the easy upper-class infection.

The masters are at home in this merciless climate
But deep in the caves of their minds some animal memory
Warns of the fate of the mammoth at the end of the ice-age;
As sleeping children a toy, they hug the last, fatal error,
But their eyes are awake and their dreams shake as with palsy.

✿   ✿   ✿

Over Birmingham where the blast furnace flowers
And beyond the piney woods in cotton country,
Continually puzzling the pale aristocrats,
The sun burns equally white man and black.

The labor which they do makes more and more
Their brotherhood condition for their whole existence;
They mint their own light, and their fusing fires
Will melt at last these centuries of ice.

This is a nightmare nimble in the Big House,
Where sleepers are wakeful, cuddling their terror,
In the empty acres of their rich beds, dreaming
Of bones in museums, where the black boys yawn.

In the Hills of Old Wyoming
For Marian
Powell, Wyoming, 1940

The Bighorns are a perpetual metaphor:
Beside them anyone's speech is formal—
Exact as the little fields ruled off like
Crossword puzzles half worked out.

Below them water is tamed early and,
Charmed in circles, led around by the rows
Where work Mexicans with white teeth and huge
Delicate farmers whose dreams are literal.

Meanwhile over them and westward long
Breakers of light crash soundless on the Rockies:
Light spumed and splintered where the peaks' cold muzzles
Explore the avenues of frozen stars—

And I kept thinking that, if faith moved one,
My love would set the whole damned range to dancing.

27

A Long Way Outside Yellowstone
Cheyenne, Wyoming, 1940

Across the tracks in Cheyenne, behind the biggest billboard,
Are a couple of human beings who aren't in for the Rodeo.
A week out of Sacramento, Jack, who was once a choir boy,
And Judy, a jail-bird's daughter, make love against the cold.
He gets the night freight for Denver. She hitches out for Billings.
But now under one blanket they go about their business.
Suppose you go about yours. Their business is being human,
And because they travel naked they are fifty jumps ahead of you
And running with all their lights on while half the world is blacked out.

Poverty of all but spirit turns up love like aces
That weren't in the deck at all.
                    Meanwhile the cold
Is scattered like petals of flowers down from the mountains of exile
And makes comradeship essential, though perhaps you choose
        not to believe it.
That doesn't matter at all, for their hands touching deny you,
Becoming, poor blinded beggars, pilgrims on the road to heaven.

Back in the Park, at the best hotel, it is true
The mountains are higher, and the food oftener, and love
As phony as a nine-dollar bill. Though perhaps
When the millionaire kisses the Princess farewell (he's going nowhere)
She weeps attractively in the expensive dark, moving—
O delicately—among the broken hearts, perhaps haunted,
Wondering if hers is among them. Or perhaps not.

Take Now This Sea
Maine, 1941

When I was very young, and years were longer,
Its badge was Magellan, upborn on brightest bosom.
That happy heister with his heart in a history book
Gave birth to continents, civilized the sea.

Later, wakening shaken by sound of water,
Breaking on lake front, or coiled in coulees,
Land-locked I lay, hearing a cold sea.
"If Faith walked these waters, faith, then love
Is not less footloose—," but Venus rising,
Love from the mist, could lay all but these fears.

And later still, startled, I understood
That salt sea-water was cousin to the blood.
The red flood circling my heart might welcome
The yelping wave packs circling Cape Cod;
And that the sea, the cemetery of all human seasons,
Still has its reasons for continual aggression:
Progresses toward an end, in stumbling dialectic:
Now retreating over the salt-flats, now
Heaving high over hackles of mastiff headlands,
Making and breaking: moving—the thing to remember.

The steel-cold sunburst rocketing waters of Boston
And the blue Gulf coiling in its endless dream of summer
Are all I know of the sea. I am here
In crowded classroom with before me students—
These are my jewels—getting and forgetting.
They haunt my hope. Else why do I hear that sea
In the granite landscape of, the tree-trapped, tranced,
The heart-hushing interior of the Maine deep?

Love in a Bus
Chicago, 1942

It was born in perhaps the Holland Tunnel,
And in New Jersey opened up its eyes,
Discovered its hands in Pennsylvania and
Later the night came.

The moon burned brighter than the dreams of lechers—
Still, they made love halfway to Pittsburg,
Disturbing the passengers and sometimes themselves.
Her laughter gamboled in the bus like kittens:
He kissed with his cap on, maybe had no hair.
I kept remembering them even beyond Chicago
Where everyone discovered a personal direction.
She went to Omaha; he went south; and I,
Having nothing better, was thinking of chance—
Which has its mouth open in perpetual surprise—
And love. For even though she was a whore
And he a poor devil wearing built-up heels,
Still, love has light which like an early lamp
Or Hesperus, that star, to the simplest object
Lends a magnificent impersonal radiance,
Human, impermanent and permanently good.

Prothalamion: Little Rock Getaway

Remember the blind harp tethered in the road?
Or earlier the whirligig station where,
Fenced with false faces, and brushing off the eyes
Which stuck to our naked suits we dined upon the air?

And later the street lamps, a row of baying bibles,
Hawked images of lust smuggled from saints' souls,
And the wild flesh rippled like a prairie of pianos
While we were booked and voyaged to our cell.

30

And saw upon a bed the naked map
Of innocence unpricked by any pin,
(Though armies were engaged) the mountains, the
   down-like plain.
And the blind harp nibbled at his noose within.

(Murmurs of off-stage voices, silk-lined outcries
From the padded cell of Europe; full spotlight
On the crippled juggler, the fairy politician:
The murderer escaping on the midnight freight.)

The harp has broken through the bars of its jail—
And at our first cadenza flared into cold flame.
A nimbus of valentines and lavender machine guns
Surround the trench of a fictitious name.

Legend

When they saw the moon would never fill
Its inside straight they knew the game was up.
The trumpets turned up a jack of hand grenades.
Obviously it was time for departure.

One went by way of the skylight and saw
The roofs mating, liquid, in a trance of despair.
And one held closely a lock of the moon's hair,
An accident pressed in an album of midnight.
Entering the tunnel one was unlucky. One
Passing the docks, had found his comrades painting
Cadenzas of memory on the naked maps.
A few, gone crazy from murders and mishaps,
Were bushwhacked by echoes in a wood of legend.

31

The survivors, arriving, did not know each other
Except as heroes. But all held the keys
To unlock the compass of the fifth season. Departing,
They kissed in an avalanche of A B C's.

Like the Watchman in AGAMEMNON
For Charley Wallant

When I saw the enigma like a blond banana
Hanging from the halltree of the century's madness
And the crazy white mice in the radio sadly
Eating square holes in the ambassador's statement—

A wolf of wind was walking in the cellar,
Scaring the birds and sending them scattering
(The ones, that is, who were smoking opium;
The others were waiting for the Second Coming).

Then I inventoried everything and found the files
Full of green carnations and blossoming glass eyes:
The atlas of catastrophe; the map of your death;
The book with the one thousand false addresses;
A photo of a man of the next century;
Five rubber slugs to fit no telephone
Cleverly lettered in no known language;
And finally the tickets no one will take,
The passport good for that country only
Which no one has discovered—

This is not new, for you have been there also
With your hands bound tight and a gag in your mouth,
Watching the moss grow over the stone cairn
While the sheriff adjusts the blindfold over the eyes you have loved.

One Who Has Looked at the Dark
For Harry Merer

Having stood silent at the window, waiting,
While the snow erases the final footfall
And love goes around the corner forever;
And never flinched, never despaired, denied,
At seeing hopheads huddled in winter doorways,
Never brushed their eyes off your too thin garments;

Hearing the death of friends without exulting
Even in secret, in the heart of crystal;
Remembering, even when it hurts remembering,
The one who got off at an earlier station;
The girl in the moonlight; the lost places;
The face on a tree in a wood of strangers—

I see you standing, angelic diarist,
And soul's historian in the street's tide-rips
Where cops broke up the demonstration
Or the hearse came by with the organizer.
I see you, a small man in last year's overcoat,
Your eyes betraying a secret exile,
Having looked on death without desire or denial.

And this explains your purity perhaps:
Not to be a part of the general conspiracy,
Not bribed with the optimists' penny candy
Yet certain as a child of that necessary goodness,
The Christmas tree in the garden of man's corruption,
You could stand like stone in a storm of betrayal,
Unshaken by the wind, by rumors of defeat.

And it is proper then, being incorruptible,
That you should keep the lists of forgotten heroes,
And of the world's small, terrible crimes that might betray us,

Corroding into pity the will to action.
It is honorable and dangerous—I do you homage—
That you have not sneered, nor flinched, nor turned to go
From the war of the poor, the awful heart of man,
Nor the little naked birds hustling in the snow.

Death for the Dark Stranger

The knave of darkness, limber in the leaves
Where the blue water blues the green of willows
And the blue geese tamely admire the wild mallows
In that always summer where memory grieves and lives,
Was a childhood friend perhaps, but now has other loves.

Or he posed as an uncle, maybe, wise,
An old head among the winds of that region,
An impartial umpire while the wars were raging—
Or he was the enchanting stranger with Spartan ways
Whose judgments were always final. But whoever the Presence was

He was cop in your county—and nothing ever less—
(Though always, in your private legend, one you knew)
Saying "keep off the grass" and "no, no,"
Infecting all your hopes with sense of loss
And to all new settings-forth crying "alas, alas."

For he is the heart's head-keeper, the bland
Insane director of a rich asylum
Where sanity is poisoned. He is king on that island,
Society's hangman, super-ego, he was born blind;
His loves are like Hitler's: upperclass and blond.

He is the keeper of what we never had,
And in order to arrive where we have never been

34

He must be numbered with the enemy slain—
His voice be loud with those we never heed:
His death alone unites the warring heart and head.

And wakes the proud blood of those fierce birds—
Else bewitched by their image in the dead still water
Of that enchanted summer where their wild hearts wither
(As our will is weakened by a crutch of words)—
So again the miraculous thunder of discovering wings is heard.

Men of the Third Millenium
For Mike Gold

1.

The season has turned over many a new leaf
Where flowers have issued the documents of spring.
And here in this square, threatened by all the city,
     The mothering grass perfects its organizations.
Indecent sparrows budding in the boughs
Whistle content in their small lecheries,
While flowering in the burning bush, the thrush
     Flings on the wind its violent proclamations.

Sweet idiot voice! Whose song, a plural music,
Sung for itself and doubled in its fellows,
Has meaning only in its comrade's ears
     And for no man here single under tree
Or hunting in the foreign speech of mates.
Bees, buds, birds—each blood has its own language.
Rock-racked, the circling Kennebec moves south,
     Losing indecision in the marching sea.

In bays of spring the blossoming chestnut tree
Fires in the night its fourteen-gun salute,

Splitting the in-shore granite in whose heart
Matching and mating, love crystallizes out.
    Earth motives, beyond praise or blame, are only recorded
Whose innocent history was lately without leaves:
O flowering stone: O light kissed voyager
    Sun circler, sun circled, Columbus of natural order!

2.

Bird is a fool, tree is a fool, stone is a fool.
    Coming along by Portsmouth, I heard that sweet bird singing.
    Far forested that song was. But terribly I was aware
In the blue air, enormously, bronze wings.
The song's green sprout was hushed as if a spool
    Of silence had wound all that wonder up.
    I recognized my selfness; sin; I put my humanity on.
Bird is a fool, tree is a fool, stone is a fool.

What set the clock and called the army in?
    What blanked those syllables as smooth as stone?
    What filled the forest full of foreign dragons?
What but consciousness, Original Sin?
Direction miscarried in that great Fall:
    Non-human history sprouted human leaves;
    And the pious for protection built a fence of apes
From any natural innocence that birds may feel.

Our recognition of Self became our compass.
    That visitation of ministering angles found
    Each human direction holy. But the world was round:
From leprous Asia we crawled to the modern pampas:
We raped the earth; we shaped the hand for a tool;
    On plains we erected the phallic crescendo of cities,
    Forgetting nature, inventing our single history:
Bird is a fool, tree is a fool, stone is a fool.

3.

Stars in the west! The cold muzzles of light
Lick at my window as I sit staring into
The indifferent moon. The moon-chained Kennebec
    Carries their calm freight; on the westward height
    The mountains are blest with it. Below in tight
And smoky circles of unnatural pride
We move through our human season. Magically balanced
    Between pull of inner and outer, across the night,

    Calmer than swans and whiter, sail the great
Galleons of inhuman order, touching parts
Nameless on maps or explorers' brief reports.
    O Unity of opposites! O salient law: to mate
    All natural enemies—to bend the late
And winter sun upon a summer course—
Divinest copulation, fathering force
    Forth-fathering Change, that mothers to create!

    Knowledge of Necessity, All-freeing Power,
In the shy mole, the singular leaf of barley
Absent, and in man, the old bird, moving rarely:
    Touch from dark to bright this midnight hour;
    And in the dark of the mind where wolves devour
The hungry seaman in the banker's street
Scatter like light the dialectic seed
    Of which Direction is the human flower.

    A few of us, our best, held that long stare
Steady as gun sights on the heart of history
And turned their faces, terrible with that mystery
    To the gentle madmen of Insanity Fair:
    Jack Christ who would have shouldered all men's care,
Rousseau who found all virtues taught by Nature,
Lenin and Marx who gave each unloved creature
    Love and a rifle and a world to share.

This is our problem, then, as the stars stand
Pale over park in the first notes of the birds:
To recapture the innocence which Nature affords
    Yet keep that Sin—let consciousness demand
    Continual fiesta of change. We understand
Our needs: direction, brotherhood, the natural commune;
Our weapons: naivete, hunger, the world we summon;
    Our symbols: the stone, the tree in the forest, the bird in the hand.

The Heroes of Childhood

The heroes of childhood were simple and austere,
And their pearl-handled six-guns never missed fire.
They filled all their straights, were lucky at dice,
In a town full of badmen they never lost face.
When they looked under beds there was nobody there.

We saluted the outlaw whose heart was pure
When he stuck up the stage or the mail car—
Big Bill Haywood or Two Gun Marx,
Who stood against the bankers and all their works—
They robbed the rich and gave to the poor.

But we in our time are not so sure:
When the posse catches us our guns hang fire,
And strung up from the wagon-tongues of long reflection
Our hearts are left hanging by the contradiction
Which history imposes on our actions here.

Perhaps we were mistaken, it has been so long,
In the fierce purpose of these Dead Eye Dans?
Did they too wake at night, in a high fever,
And wonder when direction would be clear if ever?
—For the saint is the man most likely to do wrong.

38

In any case we later ones can only hope
For the positive landmark on the distant slope.
Moving through this dead world's Indian Nation
The heart must build its own direction—
Which only in the future has a permanent shape.

Such Simple Love

All night long I hear the sleepers toss
Between the darkened window and the wall.
The madman's whimper and the lover's voice,
The worker's whisper and the sick child's call—
Knowing them all

I'd walk a mile, maybe, hearing some cat
Crying its guts out, to throttle it by hand,
Such simple love I had. I wished I might—
Or God might—answer each call in person and
Each poor demand.

Well, I'd have been better off sleeping myself.
These fancies had some sentimental charm,
But love without direction is a cheap blanket
And even if it did no one any harm,
No one is warm.

Here Is a Skeleton
The beach: wartime

You will observe on this beach three blue shells
      And this driftwood twisted and tortured agley.
      And here is a skeleton whose owner is away.
Mark in the distance a sea gull and two sails.

Even these dead things are in motion
   Mating queerly in the sea's hutches:
   Loveletterslipstickgarbagecigarbutts—
The modified secrets of this moronic ocean.

You have noted, I believe, all there is to see—
   Another ship perhaps but that is all;
   Oh possibly a wild duck, since this is fall.
—And the bright summer children? Where are they?

Nocturne Militaire
Miami Beach: wartime

Imagine or remember how the road at last led us
Over bridges like prepositions, linking a drawl of islands.
The coast curved away like a question mark, listening slyly
And shyly whispered the insomniac Atlantic.
But we were uncertain of both question and answer,
Stiff and confused and bemused in expendable khaki,
Seeing with innocent eyes, the walls gleaming,
And the alabaster city of a rich man's dream.

Borne by the offshore wind, an exciting rumor,
The legend of tropic islands, caresses the coast like hysteria,
Bringing a sound like bells rung under sea;
And brings the infected banker and others whose tenure
Is equally uncertain, equally certain: the simple
And perfect faces of women—like the moon
Whose radiance is disturbing and quite as impersonal:
Not to be warmed by and never ample.

They linger awhile in the dazzling sepulchral city,
Delicately exploring their romantic diseases,
The gangster, the capitalist and their protegés
With all their doomed retainers:
               not worth your hate or pity

40

Now that they have to learn a new language—
And they despise the idiom like an upper class foreigner:
The verb *to die* baffles them. We cannot mourn,
But their doom gives stature at last, moon-dazzled,
            silhouette on the flaming Atlantic.

Something is dying. But in the fierce sunlight,
On the swanky golf-course drill-field, something is being born
Whose features are anonymous as a child's drawing
Of the lonely guard whose cry brings down the enormous night.
For the sentry moonlight is only moonlight, not
Easy to shoot by. But our devouring symbols
(Though we walk through *their* dying city
            and *their* moonlight lave us like lovers)
Are the loin-sprung spotlight sun and the hangman sack-hooded
            blackout.

                    ✿   ✿   ✿

Now in the east the dark, like many waters,
Moves, and uptown, in the high hotels, those few
Late guests move through their remembered places
But their steps are curiously uncertain, like a sick man's
            or a sleepwalker's.
Down the beach, in rooms designed for their masters,
The soldiers curse and sing in the early blackout.
Their voices nameless but full of fear or courage
Ring like calm bells through their terrible electric idyll.

They are the nameless poor who have been marching
Out of the dark, to that possible moment when history
Crosses the tracks of our time. They do not see it approaching,
But their faces are strange with a wild and unnoticed mystery.
And now at the Casino the dancing is nice and no one
Notices the hunchback weeping among the bankers,
Or sees, like the eye of an angel, offshore, the burning tanker,
As the night patrol of bombers climbs through the rain and is gone.

41

Postcard
Amchitka, 1943

The waves break on the point, and the gulls cry,
And the sky is empty; a soldier's voice in the air
Carries flat in the wind. Afterward, nightfall—

The sun kindles on Wisconsin water,
The hills sharp as a girl's breasts,
And, farther, the massive feminine Dakotas,
The tall grain whispering through the summer weather.

The pheasant in covert in gay plumage
Salutes the sun which from the height of August
Gilds all meridians and on the beaches
Flatters the bathers with imperial homage.

Nameless figures move, but over the clamor,
The yammer of trucks, in the dark, the words hover
Like the last grin of the cheshire cat whose clever
Meaning we cannot determine, although we construe the manner.

The Spectators

The fighter moves on the runway, a focus of blur,
A buzzing bloom to the watchers, prior as a child's
First sense of consciousness. It lifts away,
Sustained in a kind of continuous miracle.
Retracting wheels declare an independence.

The pilot at one stroke moves from will to act,
From desire to fulfillment: his dream is crowned with machine guns.
But the watchers are aware of something moving

42

Which subsists always on their margin of fear
Yet always eludes them, like a question never asked.

Perhaps it is because they are denied purgation,
The necessary catharsis, being both actors and spectators?
Their climates of opinion wither in the pilot's
Absolute zero. Fulfillment is never allowed them:
They imagine they are figures in another's nightmare.

Compelling and static as hallucination,
The plane carries their eyes up and over the bay.
To call the pilot now they would need a new language,
For while their eyes still hang on the tail assembly
The prop is already entering a different world.

A Letter for Marian

I sit musing, ten minutes from the Jap,
Six hours by sun from where my heart is,
Forty-three years into the hangman's century,
Half of them signed with the difficult homage
Of personal existence.

My candle is burning at both ends and the middle,
And my halo is blazing, but I'm blind as a bat.
If fortune knocks twice, no one will answer.
Am going on instruments, my private weather
Socked in zero zero.

Sorely troubled by the need for identity
And its best expression, communication.
But the lights fail on the hills, the voice is lost in
The night of the army, or even in death, its
Big fog.

When the telephone rings there's a war on each end.
The message arrives, but there's no one to sign for it.
No one can translate the songs of the birds or
The words on the radio where the ignorant enemy
Is jamming all frequencies.

The need is definition of private boundaries:
This hill is my heart: and these worn mountains
What honor remains: this forest, what courage;
Bounded by love and by need, my frontiers
Extend to include you;

Or the need to say: this is the word and this
Its easiest meaning—for the brave words are all now
Devoured by the small souls from within:
Politicos offer the embroidered noose:
"See if this fits you."

Needed between all men and all peoples
For history to turn on the pimp and the slaver
The eyes of the poor and their terrible judgment.
Simple as the lover says "I am yours."
But not so easy.

Celebration for June 24
For Marian

Before you, I was living on an island
And all around the seas of that lonely coast
Cast up their imitation jewels, cast
Their fables and enigmas, questioning, sly.
I never solved them, or ever even heard,
Being perfect in innocence: unconscious of self;
Such ignorance of history was all my wealth—
A geographer sleeping in the shadow of virgins.

But though my maps were made of private countries
I was a foreigner in all of them after you had come,
For when you spoke, it was with a human tongue
And never understood by my land-locked gentry.
Then did the sun shake down a million bells
And birds bloom on bough in wildest song!
Phlegmatic hills went shivering with flame;
The chestnut trees were manic at their deepest boles!

It is little strange that nature was riven in her frame
At this second creation, known to every lover—
How we are shaped and shape ourselves in the desires of the other
Within the tolerance of human change.
Out of the spring's innocence this revolution,
Created on a kiss, announced the second season,
The summer of private history, of growth, through whose sweet sessions
The trees lift toward the sun, each leaf a revelation.

Our bodies, coupled in the moonlight's album
Proclaimed our love against the outlaw times
Whose signature was written in the burning towns.
Your face against the night was my medallion.
Your coming forth aroused unlikely trumpets
In the once-tame heart. They heralded your worth
Who are my lodestar, my bright and ultimate North,
Marrying all points of my personal compass.

This is the love that now invents my fear
Which nuzzles me like a puppy each violent day.
It is poor comfort that the mind comes, saying:
What is one slim girl to the peoples' wars?
Still, my dice are loaded: having had such luck,
Having your love, my life would still be whole
Though I should die tomorrow. I have lived it all.
—And love is never love, that cannot give love up.

Song

Lovers in ladies' magazines
(Tragedies hinted on the cover)
Avoid Time's nets and part no more
Than from one slick page to another.

Romeo and Juliet
Died for Shakespeare, and do again;
Yet, when the last-act curtain falls,
Survive to take love home with them.

We are less lucky whom the miles
And stratagems of sullen war
Divide; for whom Time's snipers lie
In ambush on the calendar.

As in farewell, you stand on the deck and wave
To one on the ship, and over and over say
"Love does not change for time, nor the heart ever—"
But the face at the rail is farther and farther away.

Encounter

At two thousand feet the sea wrinkles like an old man's hand.
Closer, in a monotone of peristalsis,
Its fugue-like swells create and recreate
One image in an idiot concentration.

From horizon to horizon, this desert
With the eye athirst for something stable
When off to southeast-ward—
It was a plane all right, or had been,
A shipside fighter, her pontoons floated her.

Smashed like a match-case, no one could be sure
If it were ours or had been one of theirs.

That's all there was. A thousand miles anywhere
There was only the north ocean, the poleward palor,
Like a desolation of spirit, lonelier than god.
What did it mean? They thought of night fleets
In the ghostly boreal dark or maybe
Toy cardboard silhouettes in the bleak limbo of noon:
The salvos wink in bloom at twenty miles,
The pause, the roar like a night freight
And the near misses building their faery forests.

Where were these giants? The sea offered
A single clue, a symbol; no explanation.
Northward the fog banks thickened and on all horizons
As if jealous of giving up secured positions
The night stirred angrily like an old suspicion.

Blues for Warren
killed spring 1942, north sea

1.

The beasts in the schoolroom, whose transparent faces
Revealed the gesture in the hands of history,
Made love to us across calendars where lately
They'd planted minefields around our childhood mysteries.
We fell from innocence into the trap of the State,
From Blind Man's Buff and legends, stepped into the war of the
    Thirties.
Moving among the murders to the sound of broken treaties—
Shame of our kid's inexperience was all we knew at the start.

47

Opening at opportunity's knock—
That was the banker for our mortgaged love
That was the priest for our money or our life:
All this to teach us that nervous knack
A bourgeois culture keeps in stock—
Honest living in a thieves' society.
But under the academic acanthus, among the books and dubiety,
We summoned the value of man, his loss and luck.
Now, after alarums and plots, the obscure future—
The time which is Now—places awards and banners,
Emblems across our past; the time-shortened figures
Are decorated with light which none can feel.
And now we must condemn all those whose handsome dishonest
features
Flowered on the stalk of our youth; their rentier manners
Calling alike to ruin and forgiveness
Placing across our lives their iron seal.

2.

Spotlight on midnight Europe: the furred boreal gleams
Of names on fallen monuments. A shaft of stallion's shriek
Nailed in the naked sheen of indifferent weather,
A weather of starvation. And among the ruins and the broken columns,
The betrayals, incrustations, the harps of the Nineteenth Century,
And among the treachery and hideous moneys of the world,
The Judas flags, the parliaments of beasts,
Devils with Oxford diplomas and diplomats' visas

He moved to the accompaniment of dispossessed angels:
The Angel of Love who issued no marriage licenses
The Angel of Reason with the brutal face of a child
The Angel of Hope who carried a gun in his fist
The Angel of the Fifth Season with his red flag
The Angel of Your Death who looks like your friend or your lover.

A kid knee-deep in the rotting dreams of dead statesmen,
In the First Imperialist War, thinking of home.

Home then after food queues and the cries of the starving
Lost like birds in the lord's infinite heaven
(Where no sparrow falls, etc.). But he wrote it down in his book,
Framed to remember: who were the false magicians;
What children had starved; what workers been murdered.
But what can a boy know in our time? The hawk wheels
An eye in the casual blue; the fox waits in the forest—
What can he know but the lost cries of the victims?

Down then to the matchless cold Atlantic,
Its oiled incredible reciprocating motion,
And the white ship, passage of hope, shape of return and departure
Gathered him into its hold like the sea's maw.
And the night came in like the sea's paw, gathering
The light away, and the ship, and the ocean's plunging mustangs.
By gullcry, by wavecry the littoral, the statues, the statements
The tide of the darkness gathers, are gathered into his heart.

To a barbaric rhythm of lights the seafarer slowly
Tammuz . . . Adonis, going away in the dark
With a few ears of maize, a wreath of barley leaves,
A bouquet of terror from Europe's autumn garden.
Return in Spring, or on Spring-side of ocean, America,
With the ritual wheat, with a dictionary of hopes;
Tammuz . . . Adonis . . . Warren . . . comes up the lordly Hudson
Bringing the summer in to the music of dancing light.

But the summer was unemployed that year—
June and July; and a million happinesses of weather,
Inventing lovers, filling all straights and flushes,
Knocked at the hearts where no one was at home.
At noon the roads ran over the hills like rabbits;
At midnight the clock's tongue spat out the clanging hours:

49

They ran to the dark interior, the back bush-country;
They fell at the feet of statues like a flight of iron flowers.

Those summers he rode the freights between Boston and Frisco
With the cargoes of derelicts, garlands of misery,
The human surplus, the interest on dishonor,
And the raw recruits of a new century.
The Boss's machine gun split open the human midnight
And the darkness bled its bland alarms and hours
Calling always to resistance and decision
Falling across his brief unhoused years.

3.

The bells of darkness gather their iron garlands
In the stone jungles of the blacked-out cities:
Now, after the lockout in Frisco, after the strike in New Orleans,
After the Wobblies, after the Communist Party,
After the Dorniers and Junkers, after the bomb with his number,
After the North Sea had him, after the ship went under.

The child's picture looks for itself in the old man's features,
Eye looks for sight; hand for its family fingers.
Our loves are memorialized in casual gestures
And the lost letter cries in the trunk at what it remembers.
Our loss weeps for itself, but it weeps without tongue or eyes
And the heart in its dark cave mourns. There is nothing to give it ease.

For the sea bird is not alone on the moonless waters,
Nor the fox alone in the high hills of the desert
Nor is even the soldier alone on his lone night watches
Holding with terrible integrity to his blind hazard.
The foxes have holes: the birds of the air their nests,
            and we will sometime go home,
But O in the timeless night, in the dark nothing, Warren, you are alone.

50

4.

These envy the wild birds; these, the shy life of the mole—
The blind night fugue of flight or the mothering cave in the hill.
These dream the fast fadeout, blessed by distance:
They see space as saviour, negation of form and identity,
         an underground existence.
For these ran away at childhood, seeking a stranger's country
But arrived as the masked Prince or the son of southern gentry.
These others whose progressive alienation,
         centripetal and strict,
Divorces the world instead of themselves,
         prefer the abstract
And feuding heresy. They turn from the world and find
Health in their high foreheads, or their indifference to hope,
         but their fond
Elaborate and humdrum disguises can never bandage their wounds.

These escape from themselves in the world; these others
         from the world in themselves,
But are haunted by a small disquieting awareness that nothing saves—
The explorer who escapes geography, the hophead
         who shoots up the town,
The sage on his pillar, the professor in his tower
         where his thoughts go round and round—
They are shadowed by a sinister familiar they remember but
         cannot place,
He appears in their nightmares; if they think of his name
         they are certain to fall from grace.
And between one pole and the other, as between desire and desire,
The Socially Necessary Man is hanging in chains of fire.
(His candle burns for the saviour whose birthday is drawing near.)

Oh, hell has many doorways, the key is under the mat,
And a light is burning darkly for the wandering boy tonight.
And you yearn like a tramp under the happy window
Wanting the warmth and the voices and shelter from the wild winter.

But the final achievement of each is his own damnation;
There is a family devil attendant on every private notion.
To the saint withdrawn in himself, the hero in his passage of exile,
Comes the questioner they fear to remember:
            and the terrible judgments fall.
For turning and turning in their monstrous hells of negation
They escape the glory and guilt of human action.
They haply escape salvation, escape the Fall.
But you, Warren, in the general affirmative hell
(Which includes all others) escaped these common infections
Avoiding Pride's Scylla, Fear's Charybdis, Hope's defection,
Though fiends with Kiwanis masks howled from their parlor lair,
Or tried to hold your hands across a war,
And the professors in their towers let down their long dark hair.

You moved in the light of your five angels as when the mythical great
Jesus, his common worker's clothes embroidered all over with hot
Big eyes of the poor and insulted moved on earth; or as later
Lenin arose again in the Finland Station
Thrones, Powers, Dominions, Soviets, Unions and Risings
Attended his coming and between two hells in fiery
Chains the Man of the Third Millenium stirred in his hell—

                    But the Fifth angel blows
And a star falls in the burning sea . . .

5.

A star falls in the sea. Beyond the window
The clocks of a thousand cities record their minute advantages.
The dawn wind lifts and the lawns of the Fifth decade
Prepare for a congress of sunlight. The workers awake,
Groaning to a day of sweat and statistics.

The early flowers make a fool of our Progress. The clocks condemn it.
But the lockout imposed by Natural Grace admits no scabs,

52

No hiding place down here and no retreat
Beyond the fence of apes, to the animals' innocence.
And we have given hostages to the shadowing future
(You Warren, and my brother, and the comrades
                    in a hundred countries—
In the casualty lists all names are manifestoes)
And burnt offerings to the shocking, sublime
Instinct of brotherhood, the human desire for perfection.

Accept then, brother, this heavy burden,
This crucifixion we put upon you: Man
Who was, in the university in the lost South,
And among the poor in the middle hell of Europe,
And among the strikers in the American Winter,
And among the fighters in this long war
Who was in our sin and death and at the hour of our birth
Was, is now and ever shall be
Scapegoat and Saviour.

Therefore I praise you as one of whom death was required,
Who descended into hell for our sakes; awakener
Of the hanging man, the Man of the Third Millenium.
Who chose the difficult damnation and lived on that narrow margin
While the cries went up from the poor and it snowed in the churches
And hysterical roses mourned from the bankers' lapels.

A star falls in the sea. The darkness takes it, takes you—
As the sea of the primitives gathered their flowers and Adonis,
Leaving the sea knell only, a submarine tolling of bells—
Takes you to transmutations in the wild interior uplands,
Down fathomless dreaming funnels of the tides,
To new planes of struggle, levels of organization,
And the nodal point of qualitative change:
Toward a richer fulfillment, to more definitive capes,
Clamoring loud where on tomorrow's littoral reaches
Are beached the spring-tide flowers of our hopes.

Crash Report

If perhaps you read in the paper somewhere
How Captain—or maybe Private—so and so—
Had been killed in Africa or India or even
The Aleutians—well, would you think him a hero?

It isn't important one way or another.
The guy is just as dead as Grant took Richmond.
In five years the flesh fails; five years and then
You can knock at his memory: nobody home.

For these heroes in handcuffs, out of War by Accident,
Never seem to wear well and anyway at best
Even the well dressed scarecrow or scapegoat
Possesses a limited survival value.

For instance, examine a case on record:
The dashing captain with the low-powered kite,
(It was crewed by a Christian Front mug from Yorkville
And somewhat overloaded with whisky and nurses)

—He crashed and was killed: wages of sin, etc.
While another man goes down over Paramashiru—
He wasn't joy-riding. But all is equal
In the book of Hearst's recording angel.

Yet not for us. We can recognize heroes
Before they are dead or fogged in with medals.
For heroes the hearse must be called for a reason.
It is not by accident their lives are given.

But for you, Gentle Reader, it doesn't matter a damn.
To you, real or phony, they're all the same.
And in the dead men's summers where they'll never feel the sun
It's of no importance. Everyone dies for your sins.

Homecoming

After the cries of gulls and the fogbound island;
After the last accident, the last suicide, the last alert;
After we had broken the ties of separation;
After the ship, projection of desire,
            and the homeward passage;

When the country opened up like a child's picture book
(The hills were colored by our loneliness,
            lakes by the years of exile)
Until geography began to reassume its civilian status
And the slight smell of death was lost
            in the untroubled darkness;

Then we were troubled by our second coming:
The thing that takes our hand and leads us home—
Where we must clothe ourselves in the lives of strangers
Whose names we carry but can no longer know—
Is a new fear born between the doorstep and the door
Far from the night patrol, the terror, the long sweat.

And far from the dead boy who left so long ago.

First Book of Genesis
    According to the Diplomats

On the first day they drowned the orphans,
The blue-eyed ones, in threes, in diplomats' pouches.
The dollar stood at four pounds of flesh in open market
And all markets were opened by the President,
Officially, on the first day.

The second day some opposition
Was begun by workers. These were all shot down
By students of the Radicals for Nixon movement.
Two million died in sin mortal and venial and
In hunger on the second day;

And were buried, noon, on the third day
In two speeches, given by the Secretary
Who said they were foreigners, et cetera. The Poet
Laureate was observed hustling, et cetera,
Officially, on the third day.

The fourth day was unofficial. Five
Officials of the Western Democracies were
Purchased, and some English peers. A brown rubber Bible
In a goldfish bowl was presented to a king.
The goldfish died on the fourth day.

The fifth day was the Apocalypse
Of Peoria. Armed invaders
Turned out to be a seal with a bicycle bell and two
Margarine golfballs in a birdcage. The Mayor
Had to resign on the fifth day.

On the sixth day Congress with a gun
At the taxpayer's head asked not to be provoked.
It wasn't. The Society of Atomic Widows made
The Statue of Liberty a charter member
Regretfully on the sixth day.

On the seventh day *Time* held out hope
That orphans with black-roofed mouths would not be drowned—
Or those in West Europe at least. Later the President
Took over the portfolio of Usury
And Wretchedness that seventh day.

But in the new week Congress could not be sure:
They had bought statesmen but would they stay bought?
They founded the feast of the Transformation of Liberals
But the very birds were beginning to rebel,
To sing a strange language,

And on the cold plateau of Spain, by the Mekong delta,
In hamlets on the tidy fields of France,
The accursed poor who can never be bought
Clothed with their flesh against the Pharoah's sword
A terrible infant, child of their desire.

Longshot O'Leary Counsels Direct Action

As I went into the city
    (I heard O'Leary say)
Salutes of drunken beggars
Were fired to greet the day.
While prisoner clocks on the bankers' desks
Were busy translating time into money,
Honor into thieves, love into matrimony,
The twenty best questions were never asked.
Despair, infecting the postage stamps of the century,
Carried to summer counties its mortal taint,
Through towns where the ghost-of-the-month had no house to
        haunt,
And the moon lay cold, lay cold in the penitentiary.
    O there is no love and there is no love
        (I heard O'Leary say)
    But the bastards who have locked up the moon
    Will have the most to pay.

As I went into the country
    (I heard O'Leary say)

I looked in the old places
But everyone's gone away.
Inside the correct, neurotic towns,
Luck has chopped off its healing hands,
And between the heart and the bold highlands
Hope's London Bridge is falling down.
Losing the scent, the hounds of desire in the baffling
Precincts of choice are charmed. Their ghostly bay
Chills the enchanted sleepers, but hardly shakes
In the Atomic Year, their dream of the buffalo.
    The breath of a burgess blackens the moon
      (I heard O'Leary say)
    You must smash his Fomorian magic
    Before hope will come to stay;
    But as long as someone is fighting back
    It never goes quite away.

Ars Poetica:
Or: Who Lives in the Ivory Tower?

Perhaps you'd like a marching song for the embattled prolet-
Ariat, or a realistic novel, the hopeful poet
Said, or a slice of actual life with the hot red heart's blood running,
The simple tale of a working stiff, but better than Jack London?

Nobody wants your roundelay, nobody wants your sestina,
Said the housewife, we want Hedy Lamarr and Gable at the cinema,
Get out of my technicolor dream with your tragic view and your verses;
Down with iambic pentameter and hurray for Louella Parsons.
Of course you're free to write as you please, the liberal editor answered,
But take the red flags out of your poem—we mustn't offend the censor—
And change this stanza to mean the reverse, and you must tone down
    this passage;
Thank God for the freedom of the press and a poem with a message.

Life is lousy enough without you should put it into a sonnet,
Said the man in the street, so keep it out of the novel, the poem, the
    drama;
Give us a paean of murder and rape, or the lay of a willing maiden,
And to hell with the Bard of Avalon and to hell with Eliot Auden.

Recite the damn things all day long, get drunk on smoke come Sunday,
I respect your profession as much as my own, but it don't pay off when
    you're hungry;
You'll have to carry the banner instead—said the hobo in the jungle—
If you want to eat; and don't forget: it's my bridge you're sleeping
    under.

Oh it's down with art and down with life and give us another reefer—
They all said—give us a South Sea isle, where light my love lies
    dreaming;
And who is that poet come in off the streets with a look unleal and
    lour?
Your feet are muddy, you son-of-a-bitch, get out of our ivory tower.

Soft-Hearted John's Song
    For Counting Coup

Let everything be averaged out,
Let all things be divided:
The poor shall share their poverty,
The rich the gold they're hiding.

The man who works the land shall have
A small house on his field,
And landlords (so they are not robbed)
A small place underneath.

59

And for the proud and powerful—
We can't forget them either:
Let bankers make the almanacs—
But we will make the weather.

Two for the Show

Number the heart in a hundred places,
It won't tell time at a hundred paces,
Nor the bloodhounds of hope, nor the blind sheriff's posses
Discover white antelope in debutantes' purses.

You may shun the apples of contradiction
But a compass draws an iron deduction.
There are no lights at our blind intersection:
All lovers lie on the meridian of infection.

A Real Gone Guy:
Short Requiem for Percival Angelman

> *All property is theft. Proudhon*
> *Whoever pays rent is a sucker. Longshot O'Leary*
> *Suffer the little children, etc. Anon.*

As I walked out in the streets of Chicago,
As I stopped in a bar in Manhattan one day,
I saw a poor weedhead dressed up like a sharpie,
Dressed up like a sharpie all muggled and fey.

He was beat to the socks, and his sick nerves were jumping
Like newly caught fish in the sack of his face.

He was wearing the monkey between his hired shoulders;
It twitched like a bullseye: the sign of the chase.

Twenty-three years from the dark of his mother,
From the water-borne dreams of before he was found;
Sixteen years from innocence, two from state suffrage,
And one year away from a hole in the ground.

"I can see by your threads that you're not in the racket."
Like knife-wounds his eyes in the corpse of his smile.
"Have a couple on me and we'll talk while I'm waiting.
I've got an appointment but not for a while.

"Oh I once was a worker and had to keep scuffling;
I fought for my scoff with the wolf at the door.
But I made the connection and got in the racket,
Stopped being a business man's charity whore.

"You'll never get yours if you work for a living,
But you may make a million for somebody else.
You buy him his women, his trips to Miami,
And all he expects is the loan of yourself."

"I'm with you," I said, "but here's what you've forgotten:
A working stiff's helpless to fight on his own,
But united with others he's stronger than numbers.
We can win when we learn that we can't win alone.

"Because bosses can't bribe us or buy an indulgence
For the years of our youth that they coined into gold.
Without our consent they have no power to rule us;
If we folded our arms they'd be out in the cold."

"You sound like a mission-stiff gassed up on alky;
I won't hold my breath till your kingdom has come.
They've got us in jail and there's no key that fits it,
But I'll walk through the hole I can make with a gun.

"Machinists or miners, sandhogs or chenangos—
Born in a scratch joint, live poor and die good.
With eight kids and a rupture, a wife and a mortgage,
And the years running out of their muscles like blood.

"Oh the boss stole the world and he's locked you outside it;
He's bought up the cops who patrol on his land.
He has hired judge and jury to hang you for trespass,
And pieced off a Bishop to see that you're damned.

"Put a gun on the world and walk out with the damper
And put out the ice for whoever talks back—
I may not live long but at least I'll be living,
Stacked to the bricks from the bright to the black."

Crazy as bats in the glare of a street lamp
The terrible words whispered over our heads.
Then he covered his face with the hard look of money
And nervously followed his star where it led.

He turned and went out to the darkness inside him
To the Hollywood world where believers die rich,
Where free enterprise and the lives of his childhood
Were preparing his kingdom in some midnight ditch.

Now behold him, you watchers, as he turns at the corner,
Consider his soul when he's lost in the dark.
His shoulders are high but his sick heart can never
Be padded with hope by Hart Schaffner and Marx.

And pardon his means which are those of our statesmen;
Forgive his ideals which are those of success;
Who had nothing to love him, not even a bank book,
And sins not important enough to confess.

When he's dead send the body to all those who made him:
His head to the state, to the church his last scream;
His love to the poets, his heart to Chase National;
His skill with a gun to the U. S. Marines.

And God, if there were one, might have for a jewel
The bright human fire in the soul of his son,
And strike dead in an instant the scum who forgive him—
Who willed him and killed him and never cared once

That twenty-three years from the dark of his mother,
From the water-borne dreams of before he was found,
Sixteen years from innocence, two from state suffrage,
He was one year away from a hole in the ground.

Blues for an Interim

O pretty baby put your tricks aside.
Your hair's so golden and your skin's so white,
      But the roads are out
      And the river is up
And I feel in my heart like a lonesome child.

I can do without fame, I can do without money,
I can do without books or winters in Miami,
      But in our sick season
      When love seems treason
I can't be happy with you or without you, honey.

With half the world dying and the other half dead
There just isn't anywhere room for us in bed;
      The powerful pray
      In the murderer's pew
And prepare to shake the lightning down around our heads.

Too many crying in this dark street—
You can't make love and you can't go to sleep;
    Gunfire breaks
    In the striker's block,
And I can't hear a word that you're saying to me, sweet.

O pretty baby it's a sad sad day—
There's soldiers on the hills again, cruisers in the bay.
    But until the hour
    When love takes power
We won't surrender, baby, and we can't run away.

A Little Song About Charity
(Tune of Matty Grove)

The boss came around at Christmas—
Oh smiling like a lamb—
He made me a present of a pair of gloves
And then cut off my hands—
Oh and then cut off my hands.

The boss came around on my birthday
With some shoes of a rich man's brand.
He smiled like a priest as he cut off my feet
Then he said: "Go out and dance"—
Oh he said: "Go out and dance."

The boss came around on May Day.
He said: "You may parade."
Then his cops shot us down in the open street
And they clubbed us into jail—
Oh they clubbed us into jail.

The preacher says on Sunday:
"Turn ye the other cheek."
Don't turn it to the boss on Monday morn:
He may knock out all your teeth—
Oh he may knock out your teeth.

So listen to me workers:
When the boss seems kind and good
Remember that the stain on the cutting tool
Is nothing but your blood—
Oh it's nothing but your blood.

If you love your wife and daughters,
And if you love your sons,
And if you love the working class
Then keep your love at home.
Don't waste it on the cockroach boss
But keep your love at home.

The Year the Spots Fell Off the Dice

That year the spots fell off the dice
And ten dollar bills were stricken by blight.
In the gilt mantraps of circumstance,
Old fashioned heroes learned to dance
With the iron whore of compromise.

That year in the ten best books the print
Sank under the page. The twelve best sins
Found no one who might them commit
And parsons starved, while men of wit
Looked for the word that would not sink.

That year by Money's crazy priests
Murder and innocence wickedly
Were mated. Angel-wise above
The liberal conscience cried "love, love"
And turned its eye away. Then we

Shook hands with history and the hand
Fell at our feet, a flowering branch;
But the garland of these five fortunate buds
The merchants locked in their golden glove
For a glory hand—a glory hand

Which they dare neither keep nor sell
And cannot give away except
They lose the mortmain which they hold—
The silver lock to our common world—
They have the magic of useless men.

That year we read the auguries
But could not find the golden keys,
Create the uncreated Word
Nor seize the Lucky Hand of good.
Such failures sign all victories
But that year we could not get the keys.

A Warrant for Pablo Neruda

With the fury of cinders, with the despair of dusty
Great meat-eating birds stuffed under glass, with
The public stealth of rust on wedding rings,
The shriveled bureaucrats with flag-false eyes—
Smug as one-legged guides of the blind

Or politicians impersonating men—
Water their withered bible, loosen the night's black
Knife and now on the polo fields of the rich
Exercise the clanking hounds of illusion
And oil up a warrant for the twentieth century.

They are hunting for you, Neruda. And who now
Will stop them from stuffing the wild birds of the forest
With the blue fission of national neuroses? Who
Will found the myth of Copper? Who at Magellan's
Delta remember the ritual of forgiveness?

No one but you. No one but you. It is just.
They must hunt you, because of what they have forgotten:
The name of the buried miner. (The bronze face of wheat,
The river of indulgence that flowed from O'Higgins' side,
Dries in their heads like moss in a filing cabinet.)

And what of Bolivar's tears, curling like purple chips
From the lathes of usury? They go with you to the high
Andes where police cannot marshal a true man to hunt you—
No, though the Supreme Court, unhappily sane
And naked, run through the downtown streets, shouting

That laws have become just, black white, odd even—
No. The Conspiracy of October Lilacs is against them;
The Fronde of Innocence cocks a summer rifle;
The Union of Barley is on strike, and everywhere
An alchemy of resistance transmutes your flowering name.

Such Lies They Told Us

In memory, the wild blue geese, lagging behind the spring,
Seemed all summer long to acclaim our extravagant unselfish notions
Of time—for they seemed eternal, each locked to its changeless image
On the lost lake of the past. And, under that dead sun,
Those kissing hours of illusion blessed our foreheads forever—
Or so we thought. For the years, opening their windows on
That tame image of life, promised the use of our powers—
Such lies were told us. Signs seen later made us unsure.
In the first fall frost the wild geese flew up, circled, were gone.

Nobody put us wise. There came a sound of crying
But we didn't know it as ours as we lay on the cold white table
Till the banker came in with a knife and that terrible look in his eyes.
And the judge sent his wicked little men in through the ports of
    childhood
To cut off the hands of our play and steal the ticket to Pueblo.
In our youth we heard the footsteps whispering up to the door
And the landlord's son came in, wearing the false face of kindness,
Talking of brotherhood. Later, waiting in darkness,
His gunmen coughed in the alley. But nobody spoke of that war

Into which the poor are born with their eyes blindfolded.
Though many will spend their lives, lost on mortgaged acres,
Shiver in the winds of their weakness, or, on the home quarter
Open their eyes among murderers one day on the summer fallow—
You may not bandage those wounds: allow the light to enter:
Wisdom comes from the struggle, creating the courage and grace
Which under an animal sun, in a world wilder than geese,
Still lets our eyes embrace for the proud and final time
When capital's sickly sheriff drops the hood on your face.

Fanfare for a Procession of Heroes

1.

1918. Tsaritsyn. The man in the leather coat
Stands at the CP window and the rain falls—
Which is the rain of the counter-revolution, death, poverty,
The curse of the rich on the poor. The window opens
To the east; the battle; the future.
The old gang too looks east where their time is dying.
The clock ticks, the machine gun ticks, seeding
The night with death; the night of the years with light.

'36. And the leather coat is lost
But Foster stands in the steel towns, and south
The lynched sharecropper with the tornout tongue
Documents a cruel and wolfish time.
And over the romantic Spanish plain
The blood of the Elect, the International Brigades,
Falls on the red earth, on the poverty grass and the weeds,
On the eyes of the gentle sleepers, each in his trundle bed.

Then the 40's open as a map of catastrophe:
A nightmare of islands with blood on all the beaches;
Mines like tuna leap in the fiery sea
And rains of sons' blood hurry in the May.
The fury and the heroism of those years
Are marble souvenirs of history now—
Who will ransom from his violent past
The brazen hero, keep him man alive?

2.

All the statues are bleeding in the park
In the glorious evening. The human groundswell
Laps at their feet—the citizens, however,

69

Are immune from their curious historic fevers.
Model murderers, the lover and his lass,
Go past the statue with the knife in its back.
They kiss in the shadow of a century of grace.
(Blood on the hands does not show in the face.)

The statues are the dead we murder every hour—
Lynched in marble in a public place—
Old scarecrows from the garden of an earlier time
To scare the ghosts of men who were betrayed.
And do they voice a monumental curse
On us who created these wax works of penance?
Fathers of conscience, but childless there,
They bleed with calm fury on the soft summer air.

For heroes are the scapegoats of this society,
All children of Abraham. The Iphigenias
Go under the axe of indifference. The bled-for
Most gentle virtue to its iron opposite
Changes; and the conscience-money monuments
Memorialize only our refusal to be saved.
In a fury of marble those heroes move
But cannot change a headline or our false love.

3.

Therefore we praise those who are not part of that tradition,
Lenin in October, yourself in the last strike,
Stalin at Tsaritsyn, Foster in the company towns;
But I would praise those, mainly,
Whose names are wasted on the violent air:
Fighters in ambiguous actions, leaders
Of anonymous patrols which somehow got off the map,
Are found in no index, lost in a fast shuffle.

And principally those like Warren Irwin,
Lost forever in that cold northern sea;

Boettcher, Forbes, Keiden and Cassidy
And all comrades dead in this war or earlier
Under the olives and the iron in Spain.
And also others, luckier than they,
Jody swinging in his flaming 'chute,
Phil in the farmyard with the 88's;

For Merer and Marian, for Wallant and Bob,
For Jimmy, Alan, Ron, for Martin and Slim and Adams,
For Mac and all others, either dead or living,
Known or unknown:
Insurrectionists of the Future, no tomb can hold you,
The spirit's organizers—for what have you to share
With a slaughterhouse culture, the guilty conspiracy,
With statues bleeding privately in public squares?

For all these quiet and determined workers
With their pockets full of dynamite instead of passports,
Through all the shooting and the lamentation
Bear the wounded statue towards the possible future;
Seeing beyond the war, depression, revolution,
The honey in the rock, and the bird-blossoming tree:
The long-planned wedding of the Hero and the People:
The willing bridegroom, the not impossible she.

Vision of Three Angels Viewing
the Progress of Socialism

And the first with his hands folded and a money belt for a truss
Said looking into the Commune: Well I will be damned and buggered,
Having been a banker in real life, to see how those burrowing beggars
Live without mortgages or rents and with no help from us.

71

And the second who had been a soldier in civilian life said: Jesus
Christ they'll never believe me when I tell the boys in the squad-room
That no one down there says sir, and they won't believe what's harder,
That even bughouse nuts don't want to be Julius Caesar.

And the third with the teamster's cap and callouses on his wing
Said I fell away from the flesh and into the hands of heaven
But the working stiffs down there are finally getting even
So I'll stick around until Judgment. Heaven is a sometime thing.

The Isles of Greece

The isles of Greece, the isles of Greece
Where bloody Nato's murderers come
And Presidential missions work
To handcuff babies in the womb:

Here Plato's questionable state
To savants of the C.I.A.
Is redder than the Soviets.
Its archetypal imagery,

Half underground, half in the clear,
Excites the cop in Nixon's brain;
Insolvent Socrates becomes
A vagrant proletarian

And therefore shootable. For now
A dionysian frenzy stirs
The ruined civilizing isles.
An artless and unclassic war

Disturbs the critic generals who
(Stricter than Aristotle's law)

Will not allow true tragedy
Unless man ends against a wall

Preferably headless. They
Meditate the golden mean
(Shoot one half and starve the rest)
Read Clausewitz in the Parthenon.

The shadows of these murderers through
The smoky light of history
Darken all flags, as dark as blood,
And darker than the wine-dark sea.

Blues for Jimmy
For Jimmy McGrath
Killed June 1945

1.

(If it were evening on a dead man's watch,
Flowerfall, sundown, the light furled on the pane;
And the shutters going up on the windows of the twentieth century,
6 Post Mortem in the world of the dead—)

   The train was late. We waited among the others,
   All of us waiting for friends on the late train.
   Meanwhile the usual darkness, the usual stars,
   Allies of the light trust and homeless lovers.
   And then the train with its clanking mechanical fury.
   "Our will could neither turn it around nor stop it."
   Abrupt as history it violates the station—
   The knife, the dream, the contemporary terror.

(Midnight awakens on a dead man's watch:
The two exact figures in the million beds
Embrace like skeletons chained in other dreams,
In the world of the dead where love has no dominion.)

"And then we took him to the funeral parlor,
Half-way house, after the train came in."
We found he had put on another face,
The indifferent face of death, its brutality and pallor.
"And now at last, everyone is home?"
All but you, brother. We left you there alone.

(The dead man's watch unlocks the naked morning,
And the day, already bandaging victories and wounds,
Assumes like Time the absolute stance of indifference,
On yesterday's sorrow setting its actual seal.)

Among the absorbing tenants of god's half-acre
We gave you back into the mundane chemistry.
The banker dug the grave, but the grave and gentle
Were part of the common plot. The priestly succor,
Scattering platitudes like wreaths of wilted flowers,
Drove in the coffin nails with god's own little hammer—
You are stapled still; and we are freed of onus.
Brother, te laudamus, hallowed be our shame.

(The shadow of noon—upon a dead man's watch—
Falls on the hours and mysteries; April, October
Darkening, and the forward and following centuries. The blind flyer
Locates himself on the map by that cone of silence.)

2.

Locates himself by that cone of silence,
But does not establish his private valence:
When the long grey hearse goes down the street
The driver is masked and his eyes are shut—

74

While confessing the dead man is his brother,
Only in dreams will admit the murder,
Accepting then what is always felt:
The massive implacable personal guilt.

Who refuses to be his brother's keeper
Must carry a knife and never sleep,
Defending himself at whatever cost
Against that blind importunate ghost.
Priest, banker, teacher or publican,
The mask of the irresponsible man
May hide from the masker his crimes of passion
But not the sin of his class position.

And what of the simple sensual man
Who only wants to be let alone,
With his horse and his hound and his house so fine,
A car and a girl and a voting machine?
Innocent Mr. and Mrs. Onan
Are dead before they have time to lie down.
The doorbell rings but they are away.
It is better to murder than deny.

The desperate laws of human motion
Deny innocence but permit salvation;
If we accept sentence before we are tried
We discover the crime our guilt had hid.
But the bourgeois, the saint, the two-gun man,
Who close the gates upon their dream,
Refuse to discover that of salvation
There is no private accumulation.

3.

The wind dies in the evening. Dust in the chill air
Settles in thin strata, taking the light with it,
Dusk before dusk in the river hollows.

And westward light glamors the wide Missouri,
The foothills, the Rockies, the arc of the harping coast.
And then the brooding continental night.

When I was a child the long evenings of midsummer
Died slow and splendid on my bedroom windowpane,
And I went into sleep's magnetic landscape
With no fear of awakening in a country of nightmares.

It was easy then. You could let the light go—
Tomorrow was another day and days were all the same:
Pictures in a book you'd read, segments of sealed and certain time:
Easy to go back to the day before yesterday, the year before last.

But now it is impossible. The leaf is there, and the light,
Fixed in the photograph, but the happiness is lost in the album,
And your words are lost in the mind, and your voice in the years,
And your letters' improbable tongues trouble the attic darkness.

And this is the true nature of grief and the human condition:
That you are nowhere; that you are nowhere, nowhere,
Nowhere on the round earth, and nowhere in time,
And the days like doors close between us, lock us forever apart.

4.

Not where spring with its discontinued annuities
Fills birds' nests with watches, dyes the winds yellow,
Scatters on the night its little flowers of disenchantment
And a drunken alphabet like the memory of clocks.

Not where summer, at the mercury's Feast of Ascension,
Deploys in fields the scarecrows of remembrance;
Summer with the wheat, oil, bread, birth, honey and barley,
And a hypnotised regiment of weeping butterflies.

Not when fall reopens private wounds
To stain the leaves and split the stones in walls;
Opening the doors on the furniture of false enigmas
And a mechanical patter of crazy magicians.

Not when winter on the buried leaf
Erects its barricades of coal stoves and forgetfulness;
With the warmth indoors, talk, love, camaraderie,
And outside a blizzard of years and corpses.

The calendar dies upon a dead man's watch. He is nowhere,
Nowhere in time. And yet must be in Time.
And when the Fifth Season with its mass and personal ascensions—
Fire-birds rising from the burning towns of Negation
Orbit toward freedom—
Until then, brother, I will keep your watch.

5.

I will not deny you through grief,
Nor in the masks and horrors of the voodoo man
Nor sell you in a mass for the dead
Nor seven out and forget you
Nor evict your spirit with a charming rune.
Nor wear my guilt for a badge like a saint or a bourgeois poet.

I forgive myself of your death: Blind shadow of my necessity—
Per mea culpa—cast by a son of freedom
I climb the hill of your absolute rebellion.
I do not exorcise you: you walk through the dark wood before me.

Though I give your loves to the hours,
Your bones to the first four seasons
Your hope to the ironies
Your eyes to the hawks of heaven
Your blood is made part of the general-strike fund

Your courage is coined into the Revolution
Your spirit informs the winds of the Fifth Season.

Only the tick of a watch divides us.
The crime is to deny the union of opposites.
I make your death my watch, a coin of love and anger,
With your death on one side and mine on the other.
Locked on my wrist to remember us by.

Tourists at Ensenada

The sunlight, like Rouault, draws a line
At everything, but shadow seems as real
As its object—stricter, even, to its form
Than the wasted color of the worn stone.

The sea fringes a desert. Travellers come
Where the wave repeats itself in endless promise.
On the uplands are the shabby goats, lean pigs,
And the poor in their doorways, watching the roads

Where the tourists flash past. The peasant is eclipsed
By the solar procession of the rich and bored
Who find the poor fearsome, but the blackening jail
And American motels enclosed in white walls

Romantic. Disturbing, though, that black-and-white
Life. The cripple who rasps along the street
Like nails on a slate lines all the tourist ear
With cries as real and shadowy as foreign fear.

Peregrinations of the Southern Conscience

The cynic wisdom in an angel's eye
Corrupts a ritual of lynchers' right:
Is the Recording Angel lily white?
The Baptist ethos stirs uneasily.

Is it possible that over Dixie now
Celestial light inhumanly records
The difference between black deeds, white words?
God has no Southern accent, some allow,

Though vaporings of senators, like maiden aunts,
Sugar a gallows with the Spanish moss
Of white supremacy, and liberals toss
And dream in their hair-shirts like degenerate saints.

The whore of history in the lynch tree sings
"Shiloh, and the sunken fields of hemp . . .
Antietam . . ." But a black man's neck-stretched jump
Into eternity . . . ? The statesman clings

To his myth of the Past. The pious and foolish
Dream an escape from the ancestral curse
On the Big House, their deus ex machina a hearse
Or an elaborate machine for minting juleps.

An Incident in the Life of a Prophet

And a voice like a voice in dreams cried out in the stone wilderness,
Calling out of the whirlwind, sounding its gongs and thunders,
Saying: death to the four kings of indifference!
To all despoilers of sweat and virtue and
Death to the defamers of the sacrament of wheat!
Destroy the temples of these pious sinners!

79

And the liberals said: Hush, mate, we know it is hard,
And naturally we will help you, but you must be conscious
Of the danger of letting the people know they've been had.
For Christ's sake don't wake up that sleeping monster.

And the voice as a burning dove flew out of a blue Monday
With an iron curse in its throat like the spike of the morning
    whistle,
Saying: death to the three whores of history,
Church, state, and property, and those privileged coiners
Of the counterfeit currency of life! Level
The stations of compulsion, Time's stony circuits!

And the hirelings said: Now shut your trap, Jack,
You're beginning to sound like a man with his head under water.
Lie back and relax and everything will be jake
Or there'll be hell before breakfast and no snow all winter.

And the voice cried down like a bell from the ruined tower of
    conscience,
Shaking the chromium flowers in the garden of moral decrees,
Saying: death to the two nuns of coercion
Who steal the candy of childhood! Woe
To that subtle thief of youth, the nine-armed god
Of usury whose hands are in everyone's pockets!

And the doctor said with a slick shine in his eyes
And a skinful of junk: Lie down and count to twenty.
And he turned to the banker and said: Knife and forceps, please.
And they broke into the body without warrant of entry.

But the voice cried like a trumpet from the nave of the slashed throat;
The heart leaped out of the broken trench of his breast and shouted!
Out of the ports of his eyes flew the hawks of the first four seasons:
Born from his dreaming blood was the red flag of the fifth.

80

III: from
FIGURES OF THE DOUBLE WORLD

The Several Fortunes of Jonah Hope

Here Mister Hope (or the lines in his hand)
Exhibits a love for music. Three
Several dangers have passed him unnoticed. He
Is waiting for a dark woman. Mrs. Bland
Promises a voyage on a raft of money. Love
Like Divine Grace everywhere over him hovers.

Here Mister Hope (or the leaves in his tea)
Is drenched in Destiny. A promise of power
Haunts him like Caesar, but the epiphane hour
Is not on the clock. For an extra fee
He may speak with the world of the dead: but Mister
      Hope
Is too much with the one world in which he is groping.

Here Mister Hope thinks: What's in a name?
The mystic number of his own has struck
Amazement to the heavens. Would "John Luck"
Assure him his heritage of love and fame?
Failure is not in ourselves but in our stars,
Says Mrs. Bland. The stars do not argue.

Nevertheless the fortunes of Mister Hope
Seem never to change. Locked in the pack
Forever lie the Queen and the daring Jack
Of the happy years. Oh, dearer than any dope
To an addict is that image of the past
Where all his splendid future is everlasting:

Incorruptible, there. But year after weary year
(Though he is industrious, sensitive, lucky on each
Monday with a full moon) his wish just out of reach
Hangs, like a golden apple, or a tear—
Or his life, long wished away. He cannot command
That fortune whose power was always in his hand.

Mr. & Mrs. Foxbright X. Muddlehead, at Home

Comes the murderer's evening, *ami du criminel*
And Foxbright, Mr. Muddlehead, putting his X
On the dogchewed livingroom carpet, perplexed
By the activities of the love bird and the fish in the
    deep well.
Television turns wild horses loose in the hall,
And the radio laughs while Rome and the supper burn
And a three ring circus, with lepers, jumps out of the
    wall.

Meanwhile, Mrs. Muddlehead, erotic in blue jeans
To Foxbright X, is answering three phones—
The Book Club, Christ Inc., Rebels Ltd. call while the
    bones
Of the wild goose flap in the pot and sail off the scene.
So, supper over, the Comanches enter, alas
As children, with axes, and proceed to chop down the
    lamps.
Mrs. M, lovely, smiles at the phones. All things will pass.

All things pass Foxbright. Comes another day
And the smile on the phones is the same. The children
    burn
His Sunday paintings while Mrs. M in turn
Queries one phone, then another. Hurried away
By destiny, and the need for the rent, Muddlehead
    keeps
The smile of his wife like an old man's memory of
When he was young, or love. And at last time creeps

Past smoky, incestuous noon with its straddling hands,
While the world and Foxbright wrestle. But on the
    clock

Of Mrs. M the whirling pointers mock
The busy degrees of her circle. Who understands
The world's needs but herself? And who will give
The Word? To her Club? Or to God? The fish and
    the bird
Is each in his element happy. To serve is to live.

The children blast out a wall. Like a wolf from the hill,
The wind comes in with a rush. It is bad for the bird.
And the fish. And for Mrs. M, who does not know a word
Of the language the children have recently learned,
    and is ill
With the air, and the anguish of offspring asking for love,
And evening, and X coming home, and the three
    phones ringing,
And the rich demands of the world, which are never enough.

So, Mrs. M takes her leave, as her surrogate spouse,
With his ex-life in his heart like a fossil bone,
Returns from his dubious battle, mistaking as home
The place where he lives. O, ever the fish will browse,
Loved, in his glass room, and ever the love bird cry
Secure on his perch. But will Foxbright X return
Always? The years pass. They go by

Foxbright like falling stars or Mrs. M, drawn
To PTA or a Black Mass: perilous, hurled
Like no known comet at the unwitting world
Elliptic. Cutting his orbit. Gone
To Duty. The goldfish swims. The moon
Provokes the bird. O lovers, pity, pity,
Pity them, who, in some lost summer, loved, were
    young.

Fantastic Gentry Wakes Up Dead

Waking without a personal sense of disorder
But aware he was dead, he saw the sun on high,
Light of the world, a natural. Time made hay
Of the clipt hours. A perfect day for the murder

Of Mr. Gentry, who, poised, holding his shoes,
Remembers he cannot put both on together,
That the process of setting one foot ahead of the other
Is life. But there is nothing in life that shows

Which one to put first, nothing to point direction
For Mr. Gentry, whose feet unspool the roads
Of routine destiny. Over his shoulder rides
His loosed and hawk-like soul—it screams distraction

(For it wishes to strike at the world) but is not heard
In the buzz buzz of conventional conversation,
And the day goes by. Secured beyond decision
Is the secret death of Gentry. And not so hard

As life, he reflects, while neither hope nor despair
Troubles his average day. Nothing again
Will move Gentry, whose heart in the long gone
Seasons of wish was haunted by fear and desire.

And who would have guessed that one day his loved
    world
Would have run down, whether from failure of loving,
(His own or someone's) fatigue, or because the living
Desire to enflesh the wish burns out in the cold?

Observe him now, whom only life has destroyed:
Day after day driven past hope of solution
At last at peace. Or nearly. The heart will question,
Disturbing him often at night, asking: who is betrayed?

The Seven Stations of Mrs. D

Waiting for the morning sickness of existence to pass
Mrs. D. put her head into the radio oven and turned on the
    laughing gas,
And after a briefing by Dr. Malcolm Quandary
(The noted reporter who surveys each morning's boundary
For Lady Macbeth Soaps) she was hopped up enough to face
Her great American future, and unable any longer to stay in the place

Anyway, Mrs. D. charged her moral battery and went out to see
What Mr. Luce and free enterprise might have hung on her
    9 o'clock Christmas tree.
But though the headlines proclaimed that she was ready for war
(And there were assurances by three cardinals and one whore)
Though the street was tree-proof and bird-proof, clean, shiny and nice
Where civilization and sanitation had killed all but men and flies—

Still, something was terribly wrong. It seemed to Mrs. D.
That everything was properly accounted for. Then what could it be?
Was it love? A husband and a banking account were as good;
You had the Pope and the churches in exchange for God's body
    and blood;
In place of hope, insurance; of knowledge, radio quizzes;
Of culture, a genteel sexy bestseller. Nevertheless it seemed to Mrs.

D. there had passed away a glory from the earth.
That it was involved with the packed subway and the three dollars
    worth
Of sirloin steak in her shopping bag (whose meaty penumbra
She inhaled while behind her a man in experimental rhumba
Engaged herself and the century) Mrs. D. vaguely knew.
But the earth continually opened at her feet; there was nothing she
    could do—

Poor Mrs. D—who lived on the high cold watershed
Between the few who are already living and the many who are still
    dead;

87

And it was dangerous to think, to waken out of the dreams
Of steaks and assurances into a world where the screams
Might be one's own. Mrs. D. put away the intimations of
Responsibility and went home to hear Mr. Tedious talk about Love

On television. But meanwhile the carnival in her head
Went on. The madman in her mind's house, manic with dread,
Turned loose his fantasies, like live snakes in the hall,
While the years of her youth like ghosts, her suppressed instincts, all
Like drunken spastics and cripples, joined in the riot upstairs.
Adrift and doomed on a vast and mapless Sargasso of despairs

Like a liner afire below decks, Mrs. D. sailed through the day
With her hatches battened. Oh ye who follow the historical way
To the freedom of necessity, who match idea and act,
Pity Mrs. D., who—in the fiction and fact
Of her incomplete consciousness, of too many things to unlearn,
Between the burning below and the riot above, knowledge and
    instinct—finds nowhere to turn.

Poor John Luck and the Middle Class Struggle
Or: The Corpse in the Bookkeeper's Body

The clock uncoils the working day
And he wakes up feeling that his youth has gone away.
Over the Eucharist of toast and coffee
He dreams of a Jerusalem where he was happy,
But the cops came and got him while he was still young
And they gave him ambition and a clock to punch.
O poor John! Poor
           John!
Then he claps him into clothes and he falls downstairs
And the street absorbs him as if he weren't there.
Reassembled in the subway as in the womb
He relaxes on tenterhooks to wait his time,

Reads of Armageddon on the sporting page
And appraises breast and buttock without getting an
    edge.
O poor John! Poor
                    John!
The street rolls up till his office reaches him
And the door puts out its knob and drags him in.
His desk-trap is baited with the kill of the day.
He sets it off by touching it and can't get away.
So with profit and loss and commerce and knavery
The day is passed in business and thievery.
O poor John! Poor
                    John!
And just when the mind might snap and go sane
The five o'clock whistle brings life back again.
(Usury and simony have buried the day,
The closing stock quotations bear the sun away.)
Into the five o'clock shadow of the bars
Goes good John Luck and his crying nerves.
O poor John! Poor
                    John!
At three past Scotch it is time to go home
To the little woman and the sharp smell of doom
From the over-ripe television. Free John Luck
Drops a penny from his eye into the magic juke
Box but can't get the number, as he never can now,
Because a witch stole his spell in the long long ago.
O poor John! Poor
                    John!
Then home to his castle and the sacramental beef
And after the dishes to the movies for them both.
Embalmed in the darkness of their deadly wish
The warped years fall at their feet like a dress
While snowed to the bricks, hopped up and heeled,
They throw an endless gun on their Monday selves.
O poor John! Poor
                    John!

But their Tuesday souls will be waiting in the street
When the lights go on and everyone starts
At his naked neighbor. And the lights go on.
The clock starts ticking. And the heart of man
Closes its shutters on its dreaming hurt
As another day falls into the files of the past.
O poor John! Poor
John! Poor
John!

Just Above the Battle, Mother —
(*The Death Song of Professor Francis Doubt*)

Once the powers of darkness stood
At the borders of the wood;
Now, for the devil and all his works
We have Lenin, Stalin and Karl Marx.

Galileo's dead and gone,
Erasmus sleeps in a long tomb,
And the neo-Humanists have no
Names for Voltaire or Diderot.

Where the Russians once had put their hex,
Sharing the wealth of land and sex,
Now the Red poll of the Pole appals,
And the falling rate of profit falls.

Debs and Paine are underground,
And Freedom has a double wound
But Franklin's mistresses retain
The Revolution's astral name.

The interest on St. Knox's gold
Assoils for Honor we have sold.
The liberties a poet sings
Are shadows, not substantial things.

Jefferson is dead and gone,
And Monticello's but a tomb.
High in History's azure steep
The fathers of our country sleep.

The Guardian Angel Won't Be Back

Wing-clipped and crackling with light, the blind
Angel roars in at deck level, past
The machine guns of grace, all banging away
As the bishops let go a canonical blast—

And falling like Lucifer, shot down in flames,
The heavenly guest lies dead on his back.
The Unheavenly Activities Committee
Investigates and laments the lack

Of Faith (an article scarcer than those
Blest relics that shot the angel down)
Which sends God's proletariat
Spying and eyeing and snooping around—

For God knows nothing on earth is amiss—
Isn't the Savior nailed to the Cross?
The poor are easy laid in their graves,
And what's never been had can never be lost.

Same Old Jazz

On the first day of Spring I am wakened by Blackbirds
Snapping their axles of sound on the garden wall.
Mr. Anthony M'Canicus arrives to assure me
That in the new season Wednesday will follow Thursday.
Mackerel sky at sundown; lagniappe of cloud to southward.
The equinoctial tides drag at my gumbo blood.

On the first day of Summer the Jays arouse me—
Their concept of blue grows on the wind like a flag
That has never fought a war. And Mr. M'Canicus
Has fixed it, he says, so that June follows August.
Morning moon, bone fragment; sky of machined
    monel.
Noon, pure sulphur, clouds into form like a tree.

And Autumn coppers, like a Potlatch feast,
And Winter with its diamond anguish like a snow.
The birds go kittywampus through the sky—
Let Mr. M'Canicus unchain his sundial.
Stuffed, a pheasant will sustain a mantel,
Though the sparrow punctuates an old disorder.

Order/disorder. Noon or Spring
The birds are ticking to a different time.
The formal bull lost in the baroque
Meadows of green time finds that all flowers break.
M'Canicus is not my gardener. His order
Is worse than the disorder of those goddamned birds.

Mr. Carson Death on His Nights Out

Evenings in gin mills when the band played blues
Led him to visions of an ordered life
In a new city. Night, upon the streets,
Was love and murder in unequal parts,
But trumpets aimed toward the target Choice.

Nights of terror, and a whisky tent
To shield his machinery from memory's rain and rust.
Like the lonely cinemas of drowning men,
His past flashed pictures, and he prayed to luck
That all the ships and loves come home at last.

These dreams were shipwrecked on the lunar rocks
Of midnight barstools. Sweating on those tight
Islands of pain, a Crusoe of remorse,
He remembered warnings of that treacherous coast
And dreamed of crossing mountains homeward, north.

Yet didn't. Still, the instrument, perhaps,
Of luck or grace may wake the hero, now
Chained to a Caucasus of alcohol.
Does something human echo in the wind?
An icy jazz stiffens the world of wish.

It is the world he wants. It is the world
He hates: Is it too early to depart
In the dark prime of hope and of despair?
The contradiction chills the morning air
As again the ritual of dionysian art
Starts clocks in all his condominiums.

Thinking of the Olympic Rifle Matches

Sitting Bull's ghost-laughter shakes
The hand of the marksman on the grass
Who hears the tick-tocking firearms tell
Another time has come to pass
As Ivan's rifle zeroes in
And carries off the loving cup—
Hard times when the Pioneer
Is being out-shot by the Bear.

And Davy Crockett's dead and gone
Whose knife-flash lit the Alamo,
And Daniel Boone and his coonskin cap
Have entered the continent. Texas Joe,
Wild Bill, and homiletic Deer-
Slayer whose rifle never missed—
All sure shots are underground.
A greater Marksman cut them down.

Another time must come to pass,
And soon the hero's heel must itch
For the poisoned arrow already nocked
By lover, mother, time's queenly bitch
Who slays all heroes in their time.
And now with impossible middle names
The roughneck of the future comes
As if all heroes' times weren't done.

The blindness of the hero's pride
Has driven him eyeless from the stage,
Turned all his glory into myth,
His power into senseless rage.
Thersites, practical man, destroys
The City with a formula,
While Achilles' famous sword
Could only turn Scamander red.

94

The Little Odyssey of Jason Quint, of Science, Doctor

1.

Betrayed by his five mechanic agents, falling
Captive to consciousness, he summons light
To all its duties, and assumes the world
Like a common penance. Rust on the green tongue
    burns
Like history's corrosive on his living tree.
But all the monsters of his sleep's dark sea
Are tame familiars in the morning sun.

2.

He sees the nation browse across burnt miles
Of toast, toward the time-clock. Deafened, hears
A Gettysburg of breakfast food explode
Against the surd tympanum of the air.
The roads outside to No-and-Any Where
Trigger all space-time to a zero Now.
The punctual goddess blossoms on his brow—
Pragmatic emblem of the daylit need.

3.

Now with his thought the rank and maundy world
(That lost between quanta and mechanic wave
All pulp and passion sprawls around the globe)
He stiffens, as a hand informs a glove,
And drags each lank potential into form.
Thus the hieratic arrow of his glance
Creates St. Sebastian Avenue Street Place—
All of sublunary circumstance
Crowds, on the casual platform of his gaze.

4.

Like money sealed in a pneumatic tube
He whirls beneath the city's stony floor
To where the cold coordinates of work
Advance their cross-hairs on the target hour.
There surplus value's mathematic flower
(All X squared Y squared like a tesseract
Or ghostly dirigible) grows unseen
Across the lean dimension of in fact.

5.

Grows all unseen as Jason Quint pursues
The windy hazard of the Absolute
Through icy tundras, farther than the Horn,
Vaster than Asia in their wuthering snows.
The sweat of progress and humanity
Colors no litmus in those latitudes;
In a rustle of banknotes and casualty lists
The Bomb is shaken from the wrath-bearing tree.

6.

The quitting whistle lofts a flag of truce,
And all hope's flutes and harpsichords compound
The lonely leisure. The Great Nocturnal Drift
Sets to its Deep. He walks the park. Profound
Unease returns to Quint. The sleepy lathes
Of hummingbirds machine the emerald
Of garden silence which his feet confuse.
The statues hoist, on labyrinthine paths,
The mineral grandeur of a public smile.

7.

And the world goes blank, and heavy as a stone
Rolls into night. It is the human hour.
Imperfect. Lovers, food and politics
Command the air, and Jason Quint alone,
Clothed in abstraction, like a bush that burns
In the blind frequencies where none may pass,
Stalks through that only country of the poor—
The lamplit hour the quitting whistle mourns.

8.

Imperfect. The stability of dextrous stars
Offers him comfort, but their light is cold.
A storm of sentiment, sudden as a cloud
Of migrant birds, sings in his head. Now stirs
The terrible friend, companion of his dreams,
With his emotional algebra of need and loss—
The hateful witness to his mortal part
And confirmation of his loneliness.

The Roads into the Country

Ran only in one direction, in childhood years—
Into mysterious counties, beyond the farm or the town,
Toward the parish of desire the roads led up or down
Past a thicket of charms, a river of wishing hours,

Till, wrapt in a plenum of undying sun
We heard the tick of air-guns on the hills.
The pheasant stalked by on his gilded heels,
The soft-eyed foxes from the woods looked on,

While hung upon the blue wall of the air
The hawk stared down into a sea of fire,
Where, salamanders in our element,
We ate the summer like a sacrament.

That was in memory's country, and is lost.
The roads lead nowhere. Aloof in his field of fire
The hawk wheels pitiless. Alone, afar,
The skirmishers of childhood hurry past,
Hunting a future that they cannot will.
Children of light, travelling our darkened years
We cannot warn them. Distant, they have no ears
For those they will become. Across a wall

Of terror and innocence we hear the voice,
The air-gun in the land of all mock-choice;
Around us not the game of fox and pheasant,
But the gunfire of the real and terrible present.

The Odor of Blood

Odor of blood excites
The violent, powerless dead—
Compelled again and again
To the place of their suicide,

Or haunted by the house
Where forgotten murder was done,
They grow drunk on the smell of the past
As if on the fumes of wine.

So, summoned in sleep
From his civilian dream,

The buried soldier returns
To the scene of an old crime

Where innocence and blood
Were spilled in the ditch of war—
Compelled again and again
By fury of desire

Or memory, to return:
Ghosts weak, bloodthirsty, mad:
As ghost planes tirelessly orbit
The closed fields of the dead.

Remembering That Island

Remembering that island lying in the rain
(Lost in the North Pacific, lost in time and the war)
With a terrible fatigue as of repeated dreams
Of running, climbing, fighting in the dark,
I feel the wind rising and the pitiless cold surf
Shaking the headlands of the black north.

And the ships come in again out of the fog—
As real as nightmare I hear the rattle of blocks
When the first boat comes down, the ghostly whisper of
      feet
At the barge pier—and wild with strain I wait
For the flags of my first war, the remembered faces,
And mine not among them to make the nightmare
      safe.

Then without words, with a heavy shuffling of gear,
The figures plod in the rain, in the seashore mud,
Speechless and tired; their faces, lined and hard,

I search for my comrades, and suddenly—there—there—
Harry, Charlie, and Bob, but their faces are worn, old,
And mine is among them. In a dream as real as war

I see the vast stinking Pacific suddenly awash
Once more with bodies, landings on all beaches,
The bodies of dead and living gone back to appointed
    places,
A ten year old resurrection,
And myself once more in the scourging wind, waiting,
    waiting
While the rich oratory and the lying famous corrupt
Senators mine our lives for another war.

Memorial
for Jimmy McGrath

Nothing prolongs. Neither the bronze plaque
Of graveyard splendor, nor public memorial. Even
The watery eye of memory, weeping its darlings back
Fails them. Flung like leaves on the cold heaven
In Time's own season, that Always when totals are
    taken,
    And the mortal tree is shaken,
        So, from its riven,
    Blood-branched and bony haven,
The soul is blown toward that South where only the
    dead awaken.

Nothing arouses. Shrouded in marble snow
He enters the house of his fatal opposite, under
His careless star, and the statues. The bedded seeds
    outgrow

Their sleepy winter, but now there is no Spring
    thunder
Can shock him awake, who, lying companioned and
    lonely
  In his small house, can only—
    Against Time's yonder—
  Live nigh as a bloodless wonder
In the chinese box of the mind, a mummied guest in
    that haunted and homely

Dark where nothing endures. Though the heart
    entomb
And hold that weakling ghost for a season, the altering
Cold years like snow blindfold our love, as time
Darks a stone angel. So does memory, faltering,
Kill you again—your stillness is whirled and hurried
    To nature's wilder order.
      It is the faulting
    Heart in that bloody welter
Fails you and fails. Forgive this second murder.

A Woman Praying through the St. Louis Blues

Surrounded by the casual music of circumstance
She kneels on the sore bones of poverty and ignorance.
Her goodness is common as her pulled back hair.
Her kindness makes her certain God will hear.
She thinks of Him as a vase or letter in the far attic,
Forgetting that shelf was long ago cleaned out.
She dreams she locates Him on her personal radar.

It ain't for diamonds or for store-bought hair
The man I love, he wouldn't go nowhere
Nor for luck nor pride nor fear nor happiness

(Happiness was killed in a crack-up in the war)
But for the general welfare of this world and the next.

The radio makes its generalized statement of loss
Which she can believe having buried her son.
She wants so bad, I wish there could be God.
But the blues get lost in the heavens and she goes away
Rapt in her love and a twelve bar music no angel
Nor statistic nor theory can ever equal.

Ode for the American Dead in Asia

1.

God love you now, if no one else will ever,
Corpse in the paddy, or dead on a high hill
In the fine and ruinous summer of a war
You never wanted. All your false flags were
Of bravery and ignorance, like grade school maps:
Colors of countries you would never see—
Until that weekend in eternity
When, laughing, well armed, perfectly ready to kill
The world and your brother, the safe commanders sent
You into your future. Oh, dead on a hill,
Dead in a paddy, leeched and tumbled to
A tomb of footnotes. We mourn a changeling: you:
Handselled to poverty and drummed to war
By distinguished masters whom you never knew.

2.

The bee that spins his metal from the sun,
The shy mole drifting like a miner ghost
Through midnight earth—all happy creatures run

As strict as trains on rails the circuits of
Blind instinct. Happy in your summer follies,
You mined a culture that was mined for war:
The state to mold you, church to bless, and always
The elders to confirm you in your ignorance.
No scholar put your thinking cap on nor
Warned that in dead seas fishes died in schools
Before inventing legs to walk the land.
The rulers stuck a tennis racket in your hand,
An Ark against the flood. In time of change
Courage is not enough: the blind mole dies,
And you on your hill, who did not know the rules.

3.

Wet in the windy counties of the dawn
The lone crow skirls his draggled passage home:
And God (whose sparrows fall aslant his gaze,
Like grace or confetti) blinks and he is gone,
And you are gone. Your scarecrow valor grows
And rusts like early lilac while the rose
Blooms in Dakota and the stock exchange
Flowers. Roses, rents, all things conspire
To crown your death with wreaths of living fire,
And the public mourners come: the politic tear
Is cast in the Forum. But, in another year,
We will mourn you, whose fossil courage fills
The limestone histories: brave: ignorant: amazed:
Dead in the rice paddies, dead on the nameless hills.

The Repeated Journey
for Marian

Again and again I make the intolerable journey:
First three days in the locked train, passing my home
On the stormy midnight when no light burns and all
    the houses
Are shut: then pinesmell, rain, confusion, a cold camp;
Again and again

I make the winter voyage: first the narrow
Sea-passage between the mountains where like frozen
Smoke the waterfalls hang and the scenery becomes
    portentous,
Dream-like and sullen, charged with a higher reality
Than our own; then, shadowy

As clouds in the roaring night-black ocean, islands
Plunge, fog-bound, nameless; finally, driving
Seaward, the headlands, and the crooked harbor:
    wreckage,
Spume like spiders crawling, gun-metal water;
Again and again

I climb the hill: past the cemetery, the dead
Fighter aircraft, past the shops where the great
Machines rust in their beds and know it is
Useless, useless, the night-journey inbound and cannot,
Can not turn back—

What am I hunting? I cannot remember. Rain
Slats like shot on the empty tents. The flaps
Are all closed tight on nothing. On ghosts. The night
Comes screaming down on the wind. Boredom. Lone-
    liness.
Again and again

I return to the hunt for something long buried
In Time, like the dead in the cliff-face cemetery.
Loneliness, terror of death, splendor of living—
I rescued these wounded: but cannot reclaim my youth
Nor those lost violent years whose casual ignorant
    lovers
We were for a season.

The World of the Perfect Tear
for Jimmy McGrath, killed 1945

Fire from a fixèd star
Locates no place you are.
No warmth left in the air
Reminds that you were there.
Everything you were
Is canceled in the earth
And memory's single tear
Drowns all your footprints here.

Yet in that crystal sphere
All is reflected clear—
Though no one can stand tall
Where earth itself is small
And fire is cool and air
Thinner than breath. Still, there,
The elements prevail
Reduced in memory's scale.

Sad joke: to entomb you here
In the damp world of a tear—
Though we navigate that globe
With a Magellan love.

Still, more like the Flood, this drop—
Or dead man's Ark!—will whirl
And whelm the dying world:
To raise the living up.

Counter-image for the World of Death

The land-locked lovers, lying in the park
On a corpse-colored hill, alight with their desire
Like midnight suns in this arctic summer of war,
Blind the imagination. Dream-resonance—or life—
Rings from that image. Yet how, within a world
Where every night we must bring home our dead
Can it have meaning?

For that life is meaningful is seldom said.
It is denied in court and by nightsticks of cops;
Denied in a joke, denied in dead earnest,
Though some will say "love" and hide the brass
    knuckles,
Say "justice" and condemn before the deed.
The hill of the lovers is islanded in slain,
In the blood of unfortunates.

But the lovers feel only their own dear pain.
With fumbling assurance their amazéd hands
Presume to invent each other's bodies.
Their histories, dark (but eyes see in that dark
What light they need), flame; and they are burning.
They lie in the front-line trench of the world.
Each kiss seems desertion.

But life will not let them desert. Hurled
Over the hill the voice of their violent day
Calls its commands, and the lovers go.

And perhaps they have nowhere to go? Perhaps
They are poor lovers, star-crossed lovers?
The world, which makes an outlaw of the heart,
Sets on its hounds.

Their image from my mind will not depart:
All mortal brilliance in a blood-dark time.
How commoner than salt is the element of love,
And how uncommon in this cold season
Of war! And yet the flag of all our hope
Is love, as that true country of the heart
Is anywhere we walk, if not apart.

In Praise of a Dead Body

For the savior sinew, the muscular reflex
That carried me out of harm's way and away
From the daylight accident, or darkness' dangers,
For legs that have never lagged on the years;

For the heart that leaped like a randy horse
Wild with desire in its bone corral,
And the hope that hid there; for the eyes
That have never refused to look at the world;

And for those other parts that kept
The habit of love whenever they could;
For the lights in the head's dark house, the hands,
And the bright continuum of the blood

I give my praise; and praise for that
Seven-year-old-buried face
That once held happiness—for all
My wasted body, here and there

Seeded across the enduring earth,
No longer mindful where I am.
I praise that dead man while I can,
Who am whatever he was worth.

The Trouble with the Times
for Naomi Replansky

In this town the shops are all the same:
Bread, bullets, the usual flowers
Are sold but no one—no one, no one
Has a shop for angels,
No one sells orchid bread, no one
A silver bullet to kill a king.

No one in this town has heard
Of fox-fire rosaries—instead
They have catechisms of filthy shirts,
And their god goes by on crutches
In the stench of exhaust fumes and dirty stories.

No one is opening—even on credit—
A shop for the replacement of lost years.
No one sells treasure maps. No one
Retails a poem at so much per love.

No. It is necessary
To go down to the river where the bums at evening
Assemble their histories like cancelled stamps.
There you may find, perhaps, the purple
Weather, for nothing; the blue
Apples, free; the reddest
Antelope, coming down to drink at the river,
Given away.

Think of This Hour

Think, at this hour
In the blue snow,
How the heart was cold
In the frozen year:

How we would gather,
If we could,
In the stone wood
Of the soul's weather

Something stronger
Than known words,
Than blind desire,
And to burn longer:

And found two things
In a dark hour:
Man's mortal love,
And a closed door.

The Rioting Grave

A calm like glass across November fields
Reflects the frozen moment of dead flowers.
A dying sun thickens the stubble. Hours
Stiffen to clock-work in the ticking folds
Of Autumn afternoons. Now all things old,
All things completed, drowsing in shadow, fall
Like mummies into time. But you, poor fool,
Confound the calendar and enter now

Your furious cold summer. So, though winter house
The wind-lost seed immortal you arouse
Terribly awake into a nameless new
Season—but that trick any fool may know
In time: to make a fool of time who are Time's fool.
It is cold comfort to the quick, who feel
How the grave will riot under covering snow,
Though calm as glass the winter field may lie.

The Progress of the Soul

Where once I loved my flesh,
That social fellow,
Now I want security of bone
And cherish the silence of my skeleton.

Where once I walked the world
Hunting the devil,
Now I find the darkness and the void
Within my side.

First to be good, then to be happy I
Worked and prayed.
Before the midnight, like the foul fiend,
I killed my dear friend.

Hope unto hope, dream beyond monstrous dream
I sought the world.
Now, at the black pitch and midnight of despair,
I find it was always here.

The Uneven Development of the Heart

Hardest to leave is that ruined life
We die each day. Hardest to kill
Is the sick man under our flesh who mourns
The years that are gone. His shaman's art,
Corrupting the play of the living will,

Fashions death in the changing heart
To a holy picture; each promising day
Is freighted like the old Man of the Sea
With worn shape-shifting years. To live,
And keep the murderous past at bay,

Only the killer can survive.
Thus does a civil war divide
The heart's home country. Frightened of
New seasons of necessity
The man inside is sick with love
For all the summers when he died.

De Poetica
for Edwin Rolfe

A looney clock can make a fool of time
As clouds turn ghosts, or homing geese, or gay
Boats in a lake of sun, shape-shifted by
A witless wind. That Time can be controlled
Is known to poets and to sorcerers.

They know that history, a lackwit king,
Blows books past buoys and scatters all the boats,
While drowned in bays of law and literature
A sea-change sinks a sonnet like a stone—
It is that windy beast we must enchain,

Or summoned by the blood of the implacable past
Like ghosts we slake our memory on its fumes.
Then time, which pulses golden on the wrist,
Haggard shall hunt no Greenwich of our own
Nor make our hope's meridian its prime.

But time turned ego through the iambs beat
May set clocks straight and change the current wind
That else sinks drunken boats. A ritual
Can calm the crazy king—our measure start
The possible future for the hunting heart.

That ticking engine, ceremonious art,
Machines potential to the shape of choice,
Numbers the sundial, forgives the past, and sets
The vain-weather geese toward their proper North.
Accident, defeat, within our stormy time
Are changed through form to freedom in your rhyme.

Sonnet

And when the sun, that files the points of leaves,
Unchains the summer, summons into light
Erotic innocence, proclaiming love's
Anonymous proposals; or, when late

The frost of autumn leaps the garden wall
And leaves all summer splendor in its ruin;
When, contracted in the cold, the wild
Heart wilts like a flower, farther than Orion
Or yesterday from its right cause and ground—

O love, no change or season brings us near
In the birth and death of the encircling year

Though Winter, like an annual failure, break
The yearly promise, or perennial green
Inform all April with the Spring's baroque.

Ritual Song

The primary engine of the central heaven
Solves all problems in its blue fission,
Sows trees of metal in the sacred wood.
In cold camps on the Acropolis of reason
The nomad literalists hang their worn equation—
     All is transfigured in the warring blood.

The central engine of the second heaven
Cuts the blue seasons even,
Machines the seconds to a tick of stars.
The astral bodies of the beggars shine
Above the wild Missouri's oil and slime—
     All is transfigured in celestial wars.

Hell under hell, heaven above mad heaven,
Level to level the Dream achieves its reason,
The Dialectic kills the static Good.
The gaudy peacocks of the commonplace
Die in pride of momentary grace—
     All, all transfigured in the warring blood.

Rites of Spring for Mason Roberson

In almost April when the charmed Spring comes
To Mason Roberson, a wishful green
Stylized acanthus on his capital
Column appears. It is the living sign

Of the reborn heart. The window boxes of
North Beach (where all the bilious winter long
The lank geranium unfurled a flag)
Present their poor man's colors to the town.

But Spring is owned by others. Which disturbs
Mason, who longs to make a present of
Sweet bastard April, half winter and half spring,
And shameless May to the city of his love,

The City of the World—and so to all
Those desperate lives who feel the season stir
Each worn and laboring heart with the green wish
To live as if it owned the April world.

The Troubled Midnight

Moonlight is casual on the midnight towns.
Under the starborne bridges flow
Old newspapers and ruined albums.
On the sundials midnight never comes.

But definite as casualty lists the clocks
Record appointments which we could not keep,
Seeding the timeless light with hopes
Embalmed like Pharaohs on the shadowing stroke.

The sundial has no traffic with the moon.
Nature is indifferent to the time of man.
The clocks fling down their dark commandments on
The troubled midnight, light of the careless moon.

Poem in Autumn

Time, the copper money of the sun,
That grows, pure wampum, on another's wrist,
Keeps happy even in Antarctica
Love's misers and their girls. But that fool's gold,

The pollen of the hours, is lost upon
My ignorant heart. What other lovers make
Their study—how to turn time's seasonal flower
To the alchemic rose Eternity—

Is not my magic now, black miles in time
From her. It is my industry to spend
Hours others hoard and all my summer wealth
To bring our traveling hearts safe home again.

Now, autumn. Pages from the calendar,
Like snow, will hide both summer and its pain.
I wait the winter bear of our desire
To cross the last mountain to our honey tree.

Rebellion

It was that time when the bullfighter flowers
Shake out their capes before the bulls of summer,
And down the domed face of midnight ran
Like rain the random comment of the clocks.

Then, in a religion of indifference, we
Were but the smallest, firmest heresy.
We nailed our summer theses on the wall of war:
On the altar of ourselves we praised the expendable.

The Pope of Death, with his winter Bible,
Came casting out the flowers. Like a dream of swords
We were sheathed in the broken bed of innocence while
He clamored at our chantry, a shivering skeleton—

But under our blankets all wars ended:
Which public kissing has never halted.
Small victory. Still . . . we left Old Bones to wither
In the killing cold—love's absolute zero.

Perpetual Motion

One, one
Lives all alone,
Shape of the body's
Tree of bone.

Two, two
Can make the world do;
In youth, in youth,
But not in truth.

Three, three
And the body tree
Fades in the forest
Of company.

Three, three
Society,
Will do, will do,
But not for two

Since two, two
In love, withdraw;

Wish to be one,
To live alone,

But all must come
To the skeleton,
And one and one
Live all alone.

Legend

Words I have said in anger or in passion
Flicker in memory's darkness like tired birds,
Toward midnight identity, recognitions . . .
I would be masked though I be masked in blood.

As if a dog were called and did not come . . .
Words evoke a love I had thought forgotten.
Who can forgive that thoughtless animal?
But something—scent perhaps—he can recall,

Packed in his head like letters in a trunk . . .
The bird flies *flash* the gun explodes, a tomb
Of feathers breaks above his pointing head:
A deck awash with other seasons' storms

When feathers tickled, only thunder could
Explode—the seasons when there was no blood.
God curse that Judas animal, forgive
What out of ignorance is always done.

Poem

The shadow of midnight lengthens across the world.
In the darkness only the lucky really are sure
That the sun comes up at the dawn and the birds sing
And the ones they love come back from the islands of
    sleep.

Voices of night, the metal voice on the wire,
The cry of a child, the voices hosting the air
That cry or laugh in the radio's neutral ear—
All these are unreal: They cannot make me believe:

They are only echoes thronging an empty room
Where we talked with others. Now they have all gone
And nothing exists beyond the circle of light
But remembered landscapes full of my own ghosts

And full of sorrow—full of myself. How far
Now to the farm, or to Nice, or the Ozark hills
Where first I was happy? How far to the promised
    place
Where every image creates an indifferent joy?

All that is unknown land. It is far, far
And lost in the dark, and I carry all my dead.
My murders upon me, I seek that improbable peace
After some other midnight, darker, harder to bear.

Legendary Progress

When, in the darkness of his dream,
He felt the beast scream in his side
Shuddering to be born again
He crouched in the haunted, shadowy cave.

When twin colossi gripped the East
And rived the mystical world apart,
The rage and fire of a cold star
Kindled the darkness at his heart.

When darkness settled on the West
He heard the beast laugh in his home.
The flesh sickened on the bone.
He sought the cold, monastic heaven.

When the beast was partly freed
Hunger of voyage shook the world.
Toward Magellanic darkness driven
He gyved the mystical world in one.

When to perfection of the One
He drove his cold and careless thought
The beast screamed in his terror of
The frozen heaven of the absolute.

When Progress in its cold machine
Drove all the terror from the wood
The fury chained in the drowsy blood
Convulsed at the metal smell of sin.

When in terror of the beast
He prayed protection for his dream.
A cold chaotic darkness came;
He crouched in the shadowy haunted cave.

Now twin colossi rive the world.
The starship drops its furious rime.
The terror out of the darkness comes.
The beast is raging in its time.

In Praise of Necessity

Nostalgia of old men,
That spends itself in the sun
Hunting the vanished Sioux
Or shooting the buffalo down,
Is ground-rent to the Past,
Shafts of whose vanquished years
Pierce all decadent men
To envenom new-born desires.
Thus the blind demands of the heart
Are thwarted by out-lived lives—
The Wise Man's experience is
The wisdom of killing the tribes.

How could it be otherwise?
All that's alive in the Past
Fastens itself on death,
Since to live is to change. Turned ghost
It is clothed in the future and us—
Not bound, traditional men
Remembering ritual words
Learned when their meaning was gone.
Shamen around a fire
Where tired Ghost Dancers sway
Pray back the lost buffalo herds—
Words for a vanished age.

Then praise the hunters, who
Through yesterday's cold camps
(Where banked-up spirit-fires,
Ice-flamed, will warm no hand)
Advance to break new trail
Impatient of the mean-
ingless dreams of legend herds,
Words of the old men;

And praise necessity
That frees the past of its snares,
Praising the killer heart
That makes dead meat of the years.

Against the False Magicians
for Don Gordon

The poem must not charm us like a film:
See, in the war-torn city, that reckless, gallant
Handsome lieutenant turn to the wet-lipped blonde
(Our childhood fixation) for one sweet desperate kiss
In the broken room, in blue cinematic moonlight—
Bombers across that moon, and the bombs falling,
The last train leaving, the regiment departing—
And their lips lock, saluting themselves and death:
And then the screen goes dead and all go home . . .
Ritual of the false imagination.

The poem must not charm us like the fact:
A warship can sink a circus at forty miles,
And art, love's lonely counterfeit, has small dominion
Over those nightmares that move in the actual sun-
    light.
The blonde will not be faithful, nor her lover ever return
Nor the note be found in the hollow tree of childhood—
This dazzle of the facts would have us weeping
The orphaned fantasies of easier days.

It is the charm which the potential has
That is the proper aura for the poem.
Though ceremony fail, though each of your grey hairs
Help string a harp in the landlord's heaven,

And every battle, every augury,
Argue defeat, and if defeat itself
Bring all the darkness level with our eyes—
It is the poem provides the proper charm,
Spelling resistance and the living will,
To bring to dance a stony field of fact
And set against terror exile or despair
The rituals of our humanity.

Political Song for a New Year

Gifted with prophecy and power,
All those the solstice marks with fire;
They harry out of the dung and mire
That crowd the circuit of the hour
The slumbrous, staggering, drunken boar
That on the starry, emblematic floor
Shall, tusk and tooth, their entrails tear
To wake with blood the flowers of the year.

Crowned in the surplus of zodiacal light,
The magical infant must accept his fate.
All Keepers: mother, lover, layer-out,
Are powerless with the child, who calls the swart
And southern-dropping sun against the night.
And then the blind and vegetative dead
Climb to the hysteria and ecstasy of birth:
The child is lifted from the blazing hearth
And the year sings prosperous toward his autumn
    death.

And now at the peak and pivot of a year
That saw each season signed with fire
(The mechanical throne, the burning chair

Circling the compass of the electric air)
I watch the Magi with their terrible gift
Climbing the haunted levels of the night,
Where the heroes and the victims burn and toss,
To where the Potential and the Actual cross
And the great year begins.
                              O all are whirled

Into the ruck and ritual of a world
We die to make, to sing out of the flame
Where joy is torment, fatal every game,
The only gods ourselves, and every good
Ripped from our sides in agony and blood.
Children of light, who give the future voice,
Calendar kings, be serious and rejoice!

Epitaph

Again, traveller, you have come a long way led by that
    star.
But the kingdom of the wish is at the other end of the
    night.
May you fare well, compañero; let us journey together
    joyfully,
Living on catastrophe, eating the pure light.

IV:
NEW POEMS

You Can Start the Poetry Now,
Or: News from Crazy Horse

—*I guess all I'm trying to say is I saw Crazy Horse die for*
a split level swimming pool in a tree-house owned by
a Pawnee-Warner Brothers psychiatrist about three
hundred feet above—

You can start the poetry now.

—*above City Hall kind of sacred ground where they shot the Great*
Buddha wild drags in the atomic parking lot but no good
gas seems I remember—

You can Start the Poetry now.

—*remember John Grass, University of North Dakota '69, did not*
complete his thesis sort of half-classed Indian was too busy
fighting Custer to write he wrote last of the ten
million Mohicanos when the physicists began changing red-
skins to greenbacks it wasn't

YOU can Start the Poetry NOW!

—*wasn't Gall who built all those slaveways after lifting the weight*
of the guilt hair Custer's wasn't it Gall or Crazy
Horse Sitting Bull or Rain-In-The-Face wigged him it was
later they died on the tailfins it makes you want to shoot horse-
power capitalists who done it—

YOU CAN START the POETRY now ! !

—*who done it it's between the gilt heir and the surplus value*
grand cost of counting coup in the swimming pools stolen from
the Teton Sioux first ones I ever saw with built-in jails it's

127

capitalism unlimited the american Platonic year what I
can't get straight is the white antelope they're using for
money it's the—

START THE POETRY! START THE POETRY NOW ! !

— it's the quarters and halves or maybe the whole antelope Buck that
get's me it's the cutting up of the Buffalo Bread it's all them
goddam swimming pools full of shot horses it's Christ Indians
and revolutionaries charging full-tilt at the psychiatrists'
couches and being blasted with the murderous electrical hot
missionary money of hell-by-installments it's all of us pining
and starving surrounded by the absolute heavenly pemmican-
charisma that Geronimo invented it's the—
START THE POETRY ! ! GODDAMN IT ! !
START THE POETRY ! ! START THE POETRY NOW ! !

Escape

Hunting in the dark my father found me,
My mother claimed me, and led me into light,
From my nine-month winter. In the herds of Right,
Branded and bawling, the christeners bound me.
God given, church shriven, hell washed away,
Adam purged, heaven urged, the dog would have his day.

Hell all about me with its infantry
Storming the fortress of my crying years
Could not get my notice. They had stopped my ears
With chrism of love in my infancy.
World poor, world pure, I kept my head level,
Unproud, but uncowed, shaming the devil.

And thus betrayed I fell into a world
Where love lives only in another name.

At eleven or twelve, when the kidnappers came,
I took the poisoned candy and off we whirled.
Innocence, nonsense, the seven priestly lies
Surrounded me, when, hands bound, I opened my eyes

Onto the bloody barnyard of my youth
Where the stuck pig wetly squealed against the wall,
And fell on the stone crop. False, rich, tall,
The elders judged me. The stone edge of truth,
Flint-sharp, heartless, stabbed my begging knee—
Harmed me but armed me: I cut my hands free.

Come into the Garden

When I was ten the world looked in through my eyes
Without amazement and without amusement
Noting the magic tree, the little blind dog,
The cockalorum landscape in its golden weather,
The flora and fauna of the world of ten
Frightening to no one.

When I was seventeen the world looked in
On a technicolor nightmare of sex and Depression.
Whores sang in the tree, tramps in the midnight alley,
And the farmers on the hills in the WPA wagons.
The little dog laughed. But the world to the observers
Seemed less and less happy.

Now I am older and the world looks in
On the ruined landscape of those earlier years.
Here silent figures clothed with menace move
Between the background war and the next Depression.
Frightened, the world looks in on the world it made:
And must be changed to change it.

The Buffalo Coat

I see him moving, in his legendary fleece,
Between the superhighway and an Algonquin stone axe;
Between the wild tribes, in their lost heat,
And the dark blizzard of my Grandfather's coat;
Cold with the outdoor cold caught in the curls,
Smelling of the world before the poll tax.

And between the new macadam and the Scalp Act
They got him by the short hair; had him clipped
Who once was wild—and all five senses wild—
Printing the wild with his hoof's inflated script
Before the times was money in the bank,
Before it was a crime to be so mild.

But history is a fact, and moves on feet
Sharper than his, toward wallows deeper than.
And the myth that covered all his moving parts,
Grandfather's time had turned into a coat;
And what kept warm then, in the true world's cold
Is old and cold in a world his death began.

Poem

I don't belong in this century—who does?
In my time, summer came someplace in June—
The cutbanks blazing with roses, the birds brazen, and the astonished
Pastures frisking with young calves . . .
                              That was in the country—
I don't mean *another* country, I mean in the *country:*
And the country is lost. I don't mean just lost to *me,*
Nor in the way of metaphorical loss—it's lost that way too—

No; nor in no sort of special case: I mean
Lost.

Now, down below, in the fire and stench, the city
Is building its shell: elaborate levels of emptiness
Like some sea-animal building toward its extinction.
And the citizens, unserious and full of virtue,
Are hunting for bread, or money, or a prayer,
And I behold them, and this season of man, without love.

If it were not a joke, it would be proper to laugh.
—Curious how that rat's nest holds together
Distracting . . .
              Without it there might be, still,
The gold wheel and the silver, the sun and the moon,
The season's ancient assurance under the unstable stars
Our fiery companions . . .
                    And trees, perhaps, and the sound
Of the wild and living water hurrying out of the hills.

Without these, I have you for my talisman:
Sun, moon, the four seasons,
The true voice of the mountains. Now be
(The city revolving in its empty shell,
The night moving in from the East)
—Be thou these things.

Sunday Morning Still-Life

Sun, bronze pollen,
And coffee, onyx in the yellow cups;
Golden, on white bread, the dense order of honey
Like the cloudy distillate of August light.

Now enters the breeze,
Sail bulging with flowers,
And the stowaway anguish
Of the entrapped city.

But let the breeze be still
Now, if only a moment.
Bell sound: thicken like honey
In the sun's ceramic glaze;

For now the woman with the dark hair,
Entering, lifts the moment to its noon.
Now let the wind fall,
The wind from the next world.

Now, keeper of categories,
Behold this eye of night with its yellow iris
And the black ghost of its fragrance;
Behold the amber particularities
Of this honeycomb.

The Landscape Inside Me

Here I go riding through my morning self
Between West Elbow and Little East Elbow,
Between Hotspur Heart and the Islands of Langerhans,
On the Rock Island Line of my central nervous system.

And I note the landscape which inhabits me—
How excellent in the morning to be populated by trees!
And all the hydrants are manned by dogs
And every dog is a landscape full of fleas,

And every flea is an index to the mountains!
I am well pleased with myself that I've kept the mountains.
What I can't understand is why I've kept the smog,
But since it inhabits me, why should I deny it?

Especially, why deny it on a morning like this
When I've a large unidentified star in my left
Elbow and in my head a windy palette of birds,
And a lively line-storm crossing my pancreas?

The Prickly Pear

What a continual affront!
—These spiky ears, tuned
To no particular wind,
This leathery industry of argument.

And, at the same time,
What a subtle divider:
Ears grown from ears, like an amoeba,
And the ears have it: listening to each other:
The linked and thorny syllogisms.

Until Kingdom Come
This sleepy leopard won't change his spikes:
Though the soft caterpillar may roam
Avoiding his knives, like an explorer of the moon,
And the butterfly and the morning glory's thin
Membrane find a home—

What a sticky invitation to the moralist:
It becomes almost a duty
To draw some foregone conclusion
About the soft and the sharp, this harshness and this beauty.
And indeed I am persuaded there is a moral in this.

In August

Sultry afternoon. The old dog
Moves his fleas under the porch.
Instantly light crackles
Ahead of the rattling linestorm.

from: A Sound of One Hand

Myself here at this desk.
The stars there in their own kind of cold and darkness.
Workers of all worlds
Unite!

    ✿ ✿ ✿ ✿

Summer lightning shivers the high pine.
The dandelion seed
Drifts in the wind.

    ✿ ✿ ✿ ✿

The two-faced sea—
The wild duck swimming,
The fish flying.

    ✿ ✿ ✿ ✿

Crow cry.
Darkness.
Dictionaries of a single
Word.

    ✿ ✿ ✿ ✿

Darkness of winter solstice;
And the thinnest moon,
Crossing.

    ✿ ✿ ✿ ✿

Sleepy birdsong . . .
And all the roads from midnight
Open.

For the Time Being

Coming from the Kingdom of Iron, at evening,
I jump my job-built rails to meet you on the grass
Of the human republic. Listening, we hear the grieving
And chilly Super Chiefs of progress go past

Into the mineral suburbs. Bold and shy,
Some bird outrages noise with concord of sweet song.
Daft and old fashioned. Aloft, along
The evening a bomber snores through our single sky,

And the whirling world whirls by on oil and iron.
The genius of the tree feathers another tune.
In a marriage of opposites we lie down,
Camped on a frontier between steel and song.

On the Memory of a Working-Class Girl

You run in the ruined light, bare-headed, lovely.
A stain of evening sun grows golden on your hair.
Under those flashing feet the streets of winter
Catch color as you go. Behind your shoulder
The riding shadows, misery of the years,
Seem kindly graces lured by that calm beauty
Filling your face, which at the tenement stair,
Turns on its stalk toward the wishing star.

Only a painter could keep you as you are:
Lovely and real, in the too-real doorway:
Keep you and the light from changing—like the running streets
Which under your feet run into the dark and the years.
If you could stay picture-perfect like that forever
I could forget you now—or if you were rich:
To wear the world, command the streets, your life—
But because you are not, I must give my love.

Wishing will change you. It will not change you enough
And you will change against your wishes: leaving
The girl who ran in the ruined slum of evening
For something other. Time is bourgeois—his
Best wish is for those who have—and though he ruin
All lives, both rich and poor, he doubly thus
Ruins your unwished one. No one, my dear,
Nothing can hold you, not even love hold back
The unwished horses of these riding years.

Watchman! What of the Night?

Wrenched out of sleep by the sound of the world
At your window, or shaken by a child's nightcry,
Or plunged from dreams where plane or train arrives,
Miraculous as rebirth, at the holy city—

Waking then, in the soul's dark watches,
(The child asleep now, the world run down, and you
Turning on the rack of midnight, remembering
Hope) your life tastes dead on your lips—

And it is the hour of energy's low ebb
When the sick man lets go the rope, drops down

The dark river: hour of suicides, poems,
When hope and despair drop their disguises.

And then will arise that haunting vision of life
Born out of dream or the world's need—born out of
Your need: familiar to you as hunger:
The legendary world the heart remembers.

Then you are left incomplete: like ghosts
Your dead selves ring your sleep; and all your deeds
Seem empty as rooms in a vacant house—recording
Only the sound of the wind, or a sound of mourning.

But they are not: they have a value which the morning
Light will color, recalling you to a world
More incomplete than ourselves, needing your joy, your
Fist for justice, needing your heart for the truth—

Still, in the still night, before the morning,
It is hard to remember this. Hard, hard and
All-important: for life runs round the clock;
And the world after midnight is part of the world after all.

The News around Midnight

Past midnight now, and the city in its first heavy slumber
Lies on its right side.
              The stars ride forth.
                         The last
Quarter of the south-hung moon bars the skies with its light.
Cold light there for a fact and the late and empty streets
Cold in their dark and lack.
                   Now, on this hill, my window
Is a star, no farther. And still, in this Here, I spin my luck,

137

I work my light . . .
                    here, at this table with the formica top,
As the despairing generations dream toward the day
Which can only be tomorrow, I prepare my spells and tools.

There is a planter here with a bit of green in it—
A cutting of Impatience which has just begun to root,
Some Mother-in-Law's Tongue, and a green shoot of
Leucojum just showing through—though I was a wild-rose man,
A Tiger Lily and Sassafras and Gooseberry man,
A man for the hill-hurdling crow calls and the cries of the killdeer
Falling through the green burden of the Autumn sundown woods.
But these are my tools now. These and my lonesome ghosts,
And the endless echoes of want in the lost streets of the terrible city.

Many nights you may see me here, around about midnight,
If you should look.
                    Below me the city turns on its left
Side and the neon blinks in a code I can all too clearly
Read. It will go down with all hands.
                                        Meanwhile
The moon steers and the stars wheel steady in the ultimate North.

The ghosts sing round my light. Far in Dakota now
My father is dying. And here, in the silent house, in shadowy
Rooms lying, my wife and children in their perfect sleep
Explore a darkness I can never reach.
                                        I am
Necessary recorder.
                    A voice.
                              This sad machine—
It does little good, I know; still, I am here—
This sad machine: for love.

The Dialectics of Love: Part II

1.

Why did we think we could escape
What other lovers cannot hope—
As if the flowers we smiled upon
Would gay the four walls of a room
Forever? The fatal character
Of luck is something all infer
When the censorious pall of night
Darkens the colors of delight.
The sun that worked upon the flesh,
Coupling our bodies like a wish,
Cools with our winter, wears away
In the grey light of a commoner day.
Lucky or not, all lovers come
At last to lie apart alone.

2.

The terror of the commonplace
Allows no courage but in grace—
As when from cells of those condemned
A piety of laughter sounds.
All are condemned. The hero dies
To prove the rule his life denies:
But, dead, disproves the end of man
No more than any coward can.
It is his off-hand ease with death,
A fatal charm, we celebrate;
For some can laugh, though all lie down
To die apart, to die alone.

3.

Love cools, time speeds, life fails: and we must try
The fiction of immortality.
That death, which was so far ago,
Is halfway here to meet me now;
A skeleton once in the dead past,
Now clothed in my future—that proud flesh—
He seems more like me as I change
And grows familiar being strange.
My mystery known, he hopes, by stealth,
To grow more like me than myself.
My death is fixed, but I change, I run,
(Faster, to keep from falling down)
Into my future, as we run down hill.
The future is death; shift as I will
He petrifies me into form
When I lie down to die alone.

4.

Still, in this light, I range and change
To take the flowers of the times.
A fiction of immortality
Gauds them with my living eye
And colors the four walls of our room.
Where-in-the-world is always home,
This instant Always while I kiss
And bless this mortal, wishful flesh
Gay with its future and its death.
I praise, and shall while I have breath,
This weakling love at which I laugh.
Endlessly born, not strong enough
To be the future, still, at last,
It is the strength of our whole past.
And praise death, too, out of my joy,

Whose final bondage makes us free
In lonely solidarity.
Now we must love, who are but one
Dying apart, dying alone.

Legend

Dream search
        in the dream city
                for you
Secret of laughter
        perfect
Beauty these roses of
Understanding

Find there what?

           &
all
Then fades out &
        Time
Enters

O Jesus the dust falling on that once-bright hair

Return to Marsh Street
Easter, 1959

1.

Twice, now, I've gone back there, like a part-time ghost
To the wrecked houses and the blasted courts of the dream
Where the freeway is pushing through.
                      Snake country now.
                            Rats-run—
Bearable, bearable—
Winos' retreat and the midnight newfound lands—
Bearable, perfectly bearable—
Of hungering rich lovers under the troubling moon
Their condominium;
                bowery close; momentary
                          kingdom come—
Wild country of love that exists before the concrete
Is poured.
          Squatters there.
                That's all
O.K. with me.

2.

First time I went there—about a year ago come Monday—
I went hunting flowers: flowering bushes, flowering shrubs, flowering
Years-grown-over gardens: what was transportable.
What was transportable had been taken long away.
Among the detritus, rock-slides, confessions, emotional moraines—
Along the dream plazas and the alleys of the gone moon—
Some stragglers and wildlings: poppy, sorrel, nightblooming
Nothing.
            And found finally my own garden—where it had been—
A pissed-upon landscape now, full of joy-riding

Beer cans and condoms all love's used up these days
Empty wine bottles wrappers for synthetic bread
                    . . . . . .

Larkspur, lupin, lavender, lantana, linaria, lovage.
And the foxglove's furry thimble and the tiny chime of fuchsia
All gone.
            The children's rooms have a roof of Nothing
And walls of the four wild winds.
                              And, in the rooms of the night,
The true foundation and threshing floor of love,
Are the scars of the rocking bed, and, on certain nights, the moon.
Unending landscape . . .
                    dry . . .
                        blind robins . . . *
3.

Blind Robins, Blind Robins—Fisherman, do you take Blind Robins
In the stony trough of the dry Los Angeles river?
No charmed run of alewives or swarming of holy mackerel
From the pentecostal cloud chambers of the sex-charged sea, no
Leaping salmon on the light-embroidered ladders of eternal
        redemption?
Damnation of blind robins . . .
                        bacalao . . .
                            dried cod, is that
Is that all you take on your dead-rod green-fishing Jonah,
Poor boy, mad clean crazy lad I pulled once from this river in
                              spate it is not
Bearable.

4.

Well, wait, then.
            Observe.
                Sky-writing pigeons, their

* Blind Robins are a smoked salt fish.

143

Blue unanswerable documents of flight, their
Unearthly attachments.
                    Observe:
                            these last poor flowers,
                                    their light-shot promises,
That immortality, green signature of their blood . . .
                        . . . . . .
Now, instantly, the concrete comes: the freeway leaps over the dead
River and this once now twice-green moment into the astonished
Suburbs of the imaginary city petrified
Megalopolitan grief homesteads of lost angels anguish . . .

On this day nothing rises from the dead, the river
Dying, the dry flowers going under the mechanic stone . . .
                                            Sirs!
Archaeologists! what will you find at that level of ancient light?
Poverty destroyed sweet hearts and houses once before Progress
                                            His Engines
Put down a final roof on the wild kitchens of that older
Order.
        These lovers long are fled into the storm.
The river is dry.
                It is finally.
                        completely.
Bearable

The Day Before the Night Before Christmas

I came downstairs
Stop in the hallway where the mailbox is,
Peer into that little pocket of public confidence . . .
Expecting?
Oh—a white antelope maybe—very small, of course—
Or a candy banjo . . . music from a distant world . . .
The dark looks back at me.

Outside the hallway the street extends
Like an interregnum, or period between wars.
Some kind of bird all burlap and dried sticks
Is whacking away at a frozen apple core
As hard as he can stave.

                    (Perky little bastard,
Big as my fist and brown as dung
With a nose on him like a cold-chisel.)

It's a good omen, but the day never gets to know him.
Come home at night, the letters sleep on my bed.
A bill, a bit of money, an invitation
To gin-and-malice among the mighty at a publisher's scene,
The hosts of the famous, my names on imaginary tongues that
Violent darkness crying to be remembered . . .

—The mailbox darkness extends beyond the Bear.

. . . To think these things once moved me and now you're gone.

Postcard for Naomi and Charlie

Why is it you go away
To warm a little spot of some stony, unknown city?
And why must I journey and journey
To live with strangers?

There are many of us, loving each other,
In the wintry towns of the enemy.
Why should we not gather together
In a commune of warmth and light?

Yourself there; Charlie in New York,
Don, Mac, my brothers—
At least ten, at least
Hundreds, millions . . .

Each separate:
A skin tent for the winter,
Chipping a little flint
Each day.

The Imperfect Warmth

Summer comes to the city like an old tramp from the south;
Like a drunk waking up in a doorway:
Without bread or passport,
Without maps or messages,
Without a blade of grass on the iron prairies of the avenues.

Still, most perfect there, the girls flower in the heat:
The pert tart little bitch with her switching britches,
The great and cloudy queens with their breasts aimed at the stars,
And the willowy cool ones, quick as water, awatch in the dusk.

How marvelous these scenes—
Sentimental as postcards
Arriving out of an earlier century
On the green song of the birds . . .

Imperfect warmth; still, it must sustain us
In wrinkled autumn,
In the first black frost,
In the full hold of the winter with its smoke and ice.

Proverbs of the Middle World

The perfect swan upon the perfect lake
Doubles its heaven in a single look.

       ✿   ✿   ✿

No wise man can distinguish whore from prude
When they're wrapped in the common colors of their pride.

     ✧ ✧ ✧

Some mask with courage, some with fear;
The rich wear power as a beast its fur.

     ✧ ✧ ✧

The man of conscience or the man of sin—
All shadows take their color from the sun.

     ✧ ✧ ✧

Who builds his freedom on another's life
Must start and tremble when his subjects laugh.

     ✧ ✧ ✧

When queens of love proclaim their discontent,
The courts of lust shall judge the innocent.

Magic Realism

The fifty-year-old wedding suit—
Threadbare fireworks
Beside which the company gold gift watch expends
These all but impossible hours.

That's the Way it Goes

Two numbers met on a narrow trail
"I will go around you," said Number Two.
"I will go through you," said Number One.

John Carey's Song

A few years, dozing among savages in the tropic heat—
A few years out of the dropping line-storm, on the lee side
Of linen islands, fishing on the reef of the quick wish;
Drowning, finally, awash among the sinning and prickly beds.

Then, from the niches of my porous sleep, rising
Among my sea-drowned ruins rich with the sense of disasters:
The long-past due-bills and the found stone I must eat—
The gulls cry at my eyes through sleep like the sound of the long storm.

A few years, a few years out of the line-storm:
A few counted years on the fine coast in the warm shadow
Of my most true love.
                    Now: stone, star, the far
                                        mountains:
The cold companion moon; and the old loneliness as before.

Dreamsong
a sirvente for Mel Weisburd

When I go down to that sleep
It is to the willowy marrow that I'll go,
Where the yarrow colors the heat
And the shallows are hollow with fish.

What ghosts would harrow my sleep
May burn in the yellowy hush
Of mallows and sulphur bush
As I burrow into that deep.

But through the narrows flash,
Like cloudy arrows of flesh,

Or shrouded unhallowed wish,
The bite-shaped bones of Night

And all the marsh goes wild
As the cold dead arise.
—When I go down to that sleep
I would be covered deep

To shelter against surprise
From the hollow Fish of the Breath,
From the cawing circle of death,
From the dead with their colorless eyes.

Nightsong for Eugenia

The night's long marches, and the darkness thickens with sleep.
Westward the city is shrinking.
                              Its patterns of light
Pale and draw in, like the stars thinning toward dawn,
And silence sweats from the stone.

                              What ancient darkness
Lies there beyond Sunset, beyond the satellites, beyond
The North Star shining continual heavens empty . . .

That's only an echo of my private dark, my
Seldom star-hung universe: these rooms
Heavy with lack the times you are away,
Empty with an emptiness no poem can fill.

Ah . . . To the Villages!

Leaving the splendid plaza and the esplanade—
The majestic façades of metropolitan unease—
Let us to the vast savannahs of despair
Repair; and let us seek
The panoramas of malaise, the continental anguish,
The hysteria and the nausea of the villages.

>Somewhere—perhaps where Omaha, like a disease,
>And the magnificant, brumal names of Fargo, of Kalamazoo,
>Infect the spirit with magnificant ennui—
>A baroque splendor attends our small distress:
>We dress in the grand extravaganza of cafard.

>Still, there will come evenings without true discontent—
>The sparrows loud in the dust and the crows gone cawing home
>To the little wood; the lights ending at the prairie, and—
>As the divine and healing night comes down—
>The town reeling, unreasonably content.

In the one-horse town they have eaten the horse—allons!
But soft! Here are not only the megrims of small forms
And the subliminal melancholy of the central square.
Take care; for here you find
An intermontane anguish in the wind that sings you home:
Here is a false front distinguished as your own.

And contentment is momentary in the villages.

Old Friends

Westwind sleet cold November breath:
The scarecrow
In the shivering corn.

For Tomasito

My son
Is a tiny blast furnace
That burns nothing but his mother's milk.

Little fire in the barrio of hunger,
In the coldest city in the land . . .

But he'll keep up warm in Dakota
In the All-american winter
In the blizzards at Wounded Knee
Even beyond the Missouri.

A Coal Fire in Winter

Something old and tyrannical burning there.
(Not like a wood fire which is only
The end of a summer, or a life)
But something of darkness: heat
From the time before there was fire.
And I have come here
To warm that blackness into forms of light,
To set free a captive prince
From the sunken kingdom of the father coal.

A warming company of the cold-blooded—
These carbon serpents of bituminous gardens,
These inflammable tunnels of dead song from the black pit,
This sparkling end of the great beasts, these blazing
Stone flowers diamond fire incandescent fruit.
And out of all that death, now,
At midnight, my love and I are riding
Down the old high roads of inexhaustible light.

151

The Cold Heart

The crowbar I lost at winterset—
I turned my back and it slipped away
Its curlicue masked in the masquerade
Where the blizzard whirled the early snow—

I found it: after the rain of spring,
Skulking beneath the new year grass.
An echo of winter chilled my palm
And lived till June in the ungenerous iron.

Salute

The wind is driving its frayed buffalo from north of the mountain.
Birds clench on a bough like hands nesting in coatsleeves
Against the cold. Horizon-line electric talk of the storm.
Rainy dark. Cold. Afternoon. Autumn.

Later, a boy, shoes awash in the runaway gutter,
Draws, on the thinnest string, like a swatch of invincible sunlight,
His drenched collapsing kite from the cold well of the sky.

Landscape with Birds

Alternate acres of loud song and silence—
Larks rising out of the dead spring bunch-grass,
Out of cattle bones and brown cow chips
Larks rising always ahead of me
As I walk on the coulee slope:
Song and then silence, silence
And song.

152

I whistled into the dead calm
To gull a simple mile of larks and the birds whirred quarreling
Into the sun.
              Static of dry grass; the bright bones honeycombed
With ancient quiet. Beyond: the heart-stilling hush of the prairie.

The birds came back.
                     I walked all morning on that quilt
Of birds and bones,
One lark ahead of silence, behind that frontier of song.

Hoot!

1.

Something lights my way
In the soft country of the future—
Like one hundred sixty acres
Of buried
Owls.

2.

I'm journeying, in darkness journeying . . .
And for my light
Only a sackful
Of imperfect (sleepy)
Owls.

3.

Sometimes I really see—
Like an owl here,
An owl
There.

For Alvaro

The unseen frog:
Green moss, obsidian
    pure water
        skin-smooth pale stone
All, invented
In the deep well
Of your song.

For Eugenia

Coming back at night to the late and empty house,
I found the rooms colder because you were away,
The soup misses you, my girl,
The squash is forlorn in the garden,
And the news in the morning paper
Is already several years old.

from: A Sound of One Hand

After moondown
I hear the hot-month corn stretching its joints.
A distant coyote.
This growing peace.

          ❁ ❁ ❁ ❁

The leaves are burnt by the frost.
In still autumn the cry of wild geese
Freezes the moonlight.

          ❁ ❁ ❁ ❁

Cauliflower, and the buddha-like seeds of the pepper
Turning their prayerwheels in the green gloom of their caves.
All these we praise: they please us all ways: these smallest virtues.
All these earth-given:
                    and the heaven-hung fruit also . . .
                                        As instance
Banana which continually makes angelic ears out of sour
Purses, or the winy abacus of the holy grape on its cross
Of alcohol, or the peach with its fur like a young girl's—
All these we praise: the winter in the flesh of the apple, and the sun
Domesticated under the orange's rind.
                        We praise
By the skin of our teeth, Persimmon, and Pawpaw's constant
Affair with gravity, and the proletariat of the pomegranate
Inside its leathery city.
                    And let us praise all these
As they please us: skin, flesh, flower, and the flowering
Bones of their seeds: from which come orchards: bees: honey:
Flowers, love's language, love, heart's ease, poems, praise.

Evening Prayers

ow I lay me down to sleep.
ray the Mighty peace to keep.

t They let neither fire nor bomb
  me dreaming to kingdom come.

hat His surplus value will
nly sweat and leave my soul.

lease, Sir, give me these.
ur ancient liberties.

A friend calls, saying:
"I have a new poem."

❖   ❖   ❖   ❖

Forlorn crows
In the rotting February snow
Franz Joseph Land
                I remember
The polar rectitudes.

The Deer in the Ditch

We saw him there in the dry season among the burning
Daisies. Knocked off the road by a car, neck broke, his haunch
Open like a book of flesh.
                    Slack center of the day's eye,
He flashed still for the flies to gloss him into the dark.

Many were the losses on the roads that year my brother was dying,
Chair-broken, geared to his death, wheeling toward night while
The C.I.A. killed Cubans.
                    Dead Reds. Dear brothers. Deer
In the ditch.
            Tokens . . .
                    so much steel and so little breath.

These passings like fictions have nothing to do with each other.
Going back there in the fast sun of the new-summer fact,
I read the right of way, seeking a sign in the ditch, convention
Of wild flowers maybe (where the bone went home) enriched by mild
    flesh.

But there are no evidences of such deaths.

Obituary

Sixty years at hard labor
In the stony fields of his country!

I think of buffalo bones,
Broken hame straps,
Tractors rusting beside the abandoned farmhouse.

Used Up

1.

I remember the new-dropped colts in the time when I was a boy:
The steam of their bodies in the cold morning like a visible soul,
And the crimped hairy ring of warmed grass, first circle of sleep.
Spider-legged, later, they ate sugar from my shaken, scary hand.

2.

In a few more years they were broken: their necks were circled
With a farmer's need: with the dead leather legends and collars
                                 of their kin.
Gelded, the wild years cut out of them, harnessed to the world,
They walk the bright days' black furrows and gilded seasons of use.

3.

Now, dead; swung from the haymow track with block and tackle:
Gut-slit, blood in a tub for pigs, their skin dragged over
Their heads by a team of mules. Circlet of crows:
                        coyote song:
                           and bones

Rusting coulee moonlight: lush greenest spring grass where the body
Leaped.
                Three acts and death.
                          The horse
                                    rides
Into the earth.

Praises

The vegetables please us with their modes and virtues.
                                  The demure heart
Of the lettuce inside its circular court, baroque ear
Of quiet under its rustling house of lace, pleases
Us.
        And the bold strength of the celery, its green Hispanic
¡Shout! its exclamatory confetti.
                         And the analogue that is Oni
Ptolemaic astronomy and tearful allegory, the Platonic circles
Of His inexhaustible soul!
                  O and the straightforwardness
In the labyrinth of Cabbage, the infallible recitude of Ho

Under its cone of silence like a papal hat—
                        All thes
Please us.
        And the syllabus of the corn,
                      that war

Roads leading out of the wigwams of its silky
The nobility of the dill, cool in its silences a
Tomatoes five-alarm fires in their musky bar
Asleep in their cartridge clips,
                    beetsblood

A Sixth Heresy of Parson Chance

To strong men flat upon their backs,
Any dwarf looks bunyanesque:
The idiot with *love* to parse
Seems wiser than an odalisque
To eunuchs, and the verb *to find*
Is lost in the countries of the blind.

The issue of the bloodless men
In a whinnying and war-like clamor;
Faster than compound interest
Awakens General Doppelganger—
The Pope of Oil, the Editor's Whore
Trumpet the masters' man to war.

The crooked and concupiscent,
And the man-with-the-bull-ring-in-his-nose
Praise a roman circus where
Only the poor must pay. The rose
Is thornless; fire chills; man is free.
And the fish are harping in the sea.

Mottoes for a Sampler on Historical Subjects

The Puritans at Plymouth stayed
Drunk all year in the tropic weather.
They set their phallic may-poles up
And danced all night with Increase Mather.
    And thus, says Michael Wigglesworth,
    The Pagan Fathers brought to birth
    The freest culture known on earth.

159

Johnny Appleseed one day
Took Washington across his knee
And whaled the living daylights out
For chopping down the cherry tree.
　　The national history thus is one
　　Of democratic action,
　　Says Sylvan S. Historian.

Through Uncas and Geronimo
The War of the Elect was won,
And wage and chattel slaves were freed
Following Shays' Rebellion.
　　So we unite all principles,
　　With profane Greek and Talmud skills,
　　Says the sweet singer of General Mills.

Haywood, the Peoples' Commissar,
After the Diet of Wounded Knee,
Adopted the theses of Joe Hill,
The Delegate for Poetry.
　　So history proves what we all knew:
　　We're revolutionary too,
　　Croons the Partisan Review.

Then why does each madhouse, every jail
Fill up while through th' indifferent sky
(Where glow the heavens with last steps of day)
The bombers and the generals fly?
　　Bemused across the campus grass,
　　Seeing darkly, as through a glass,
　　The earnest history students pass.

Song for an Armistice Day

Wash the eye with slogans now,
Bedeck the heart with candy flags.
Let yellowing admirals in full blue rigs
And generals appear. (The wooden legs
Of the wounded know more than the generals know.)

Then bugles embrace with a duelling sound,
And Bibles are thumped in the house of the Word:
"Though their armies are mighty, we'll beat them. God
Is with us." (Of purple hearts, the blood
Is deeper than admirals ever drowned.)

The hosannas and hubba-hubba's cease—
The commanders dry up and blow off in their cars.
The vets limp home to inveterate wars
With wounds reopened. (Army stores
Have medals for everything but peace.)

The grave is deserted. Women mourn,
Hunting you back in the furry dark,
But cannot recall you: can hate the work
That stripped you of flesh and flung soul forth.
(If the generals see it, they'll shoot it down.)

So your little light, in the dark press
Of the callous and patriot night that palls
On you and the world, is reburied. (All
Memorials propitiate accusing, tall,
Dead heros who living might curse, not bless.)

After the Beat Generation

I.

What! All those years after the Annunciation at Venice
And no revolution in sight?
                              And how long since the lads
From West Stud Horse Texas and Poontang-on-the-Hudson
Slogged through the city of Lost Angels in the beardless years
Led by a cloud no bigger than an orgone box, whence issued—
Promising, promising, promising (and no revolution and no
Revolution in sight) issued the cash-tongued summons
Toward the guru of Big Sur and San Fran's stammering Apocalypse?

I do not know how long this thing can go on!
—Waiting for Lefty, waiting for Godot, waiting for the heavenly fix.
In my way of counting, time comes in through my skin—
Blind Cosmos Alley, charismatic light
Of electric mustaches in the Deep Night of the Gashouse gunfire
From enormous imaginary loud cap pistols of infinitely small caliber
Anarcholunacy—how long, in that light, to read what signposts?
When all that glows with a gem-like flame is the end of Lipton's cigar?

II.

There ought to be other ways to skin this cat:
Journeys through the deep snow of a black book, bonefire, and
    wormlight
To burn through the salty moss to the mark on the blazed tree.
How long now since love out of a cloud of flesh
In Elysian Park stammered your secret name? Since Curtis
Zahn dipped his beard in the radioactive sea?
Since Rolfe went underground for the last time in that boneyard
On Santa Monica?
                    Bench marks.
                              Sea anchors of drowned guitars.

162

Alas, compañeros, have we not seen the imaginary travellers—
Whole boatloads of sensitive boy scouts aground in the dead river
Of the Lost Angels, and the coffee shops' simple malfeasance of Light?
Hence it is required of us to go forward over the rubber bones
Of these synthetic rebels, over the tame poets
Who came to the Time's big table and the harp-shaped evergreen
                                    swimming pools
To drink the waters of darkness.
                        In the Carbon 14 dating
We find the Naked Man: the starving: the Moon in the Penitentiary.

All The Dead Poets

How vainly men themselves bestir
For Bollingen or Pulitzer,
To raise, through ritual and rhyme
Some Lazarus of an earlier time:
The thought that died upon the page;
The attitude stiffened with its age;
The feeling, once appropriate,
Now, like honesty, out of date;
The elegant tone elegiac
That embalms the venom of a hack—
All the outmoded consciousness
A timid reason can assess:
His sin that in the soul's dark night
Like an ancient cod's head gives off light—
All of this some will sing or say
(As if God's death were but a play)—
All the dead poets of the day.

II. Random Roderick

Here's one who sings (as he were wood)
The *angst* he has best understood:
What the Ash and Hickory
Feel toward Life and Poetry.
Of what the Willow should or shouldn't
He warbles his native wood-note prudent,
Proclaiming so everyone may know it
He's every ring the old oaken poet.
"Poems are made by fools like me
But only God can make a tree,"
Said Kilmer. Roderick proves the rule:
Too many trees may make a fool.
For there's a kind of Sallic law:
Such willowy whimsy is a bore.
Still, better his light than heavy work—
His agenbite's worse than his bark.

Earnest at his vatic trade,
He studies to be nobly mad;
Courts furor poeticus
(So long as it is decorous)
Thinking, when he has beguiled
The critic-beasts, to mount the wild
Pegasus of mantic verse—
If only someone holds the horse.
Yet to be "lyrically wild"
(And simple as a little child)
Is not enough. The art of sinking
Is not enough: he must be thinking—

Thinking, thinking all the while
(As a history doctor will)
Thinking, thinking all the day,
While the cute ideas play,

And when the hunting thoughts come home—
Lo! they've bagged another poem!
This philosophic poet's bold—
Proudly demands his right to hold
Such attitudes to church and state
As died in 1848.
Built from ruin and decay
His dome of many-colored clay
Arises—O Philosophy,
Can this jakes thy mansion be?
Wilt thou number in thy van
This shambling nineteenth century man?

Meanwhile our poet is romancing
And sets the small ideas dancing:
His poems would rather mean than be—
O Wouldsman, Wouldsman, spare that tree!

The Defeat of the Novelist

Waiting for his characters to grow
He brooded on his first novel for ten
Years by that time his hero had grand
Children and (while the Novelist—like—
Sometimes—Homer? slept) had put on seven
Hundred and sixty-five and a quarter
Pounds it was discouraging neverthe
Less the Novelist decided he could
Turn him into a trilogy but now
And again muttered something in his sleep
Some—"forty-five" (grandchildren?) "stoned"—something

The second book was easier except
For the pigeons they were everywhere they
Were good for nothing they were furry white

Imaginary pigeons he hope to
Eat some but they never come down off the
Roof his hero had turned to a pigeon
Fancier eventually it was
Too much the Novelist push him off the
Ledge he fall all the way through the sixteenth
Chapter seven hundred sixty five lbs. of
Him the Novelist give up using
Pillows

It was in the third book that the Trouble
Came (it turn out that the hero, caught on
A fourth-story clothesline from chapter five
Still lives great Bird) it was in the third book
Our hero was analyzed he lost nine
Hundred and nine and a quarter pounds in-
Stantly no longer a slob but a pure
Bastard he began to put on airs sick
Airs his dreams gave the Novelist nightmares
Night mares of a special kind because our
Hero's analyst an existential
Jungian was going through a Zen phase
Of the beat variety it's all been
Recorded in Venice

To make these matters monumentally
Worse his hero whose name is Larry or
Harry decided he is one of Jung's
Archetypal images a centaur in fact
He enter himself at Santa Anita
Which wouldn't have been so bad except he
Run out of the money he do not fail
To put all of the Novelist's money down

It was the last straw it was a bad day
For Dostoyevesky for American
Letters for Johnny Longden

Driving Toward Boston I Run Across
One of Robert Bly's Old Poems

1.

Tonight we are driving past Lac Qui Parle toward Boston.
When I think of the Boston ladies I am suddenly galvanic with joy!
I see them lying there, pale with Love . . . like flowers . . . like
   palimpsests!
On which we can still make out a few marginal words . . .
Wampum . . . rackrent . . . pui ine o dromos sto horyo, asshole!
Ah—the lemon ladies and the lime-green ladies of Boston!

2.

The parlors of those houses on the road to Boston are full of salt.
These ladies have taken the sea to bed just once too often . . .
And the men— ah, here the Cabots and the Lodges and Lowells
   are dozing
(Dreaming of rum and molasses, dreaming of Sacco and Vanzetti)
In an oily torpor, like the sleep of ancient Cadillacs . . .
Alas! John Adams: desuetude has entered the timing-chains of those
   enormous engines!

3.

Driving toward Boston we pass the Stuffed Ski Surf Shop—
And then the Stuffed Ski Surf Shop—again and again!
Perhaps we are not driving toward Boston after all . . .
Waltham flies by, full of mysterious time zones . . .
I know Boston is on the Post Road someplace in the nineteenth century.
The wind is whistling a snatch in the puritan winefield.
I speed forward, confident, thinking of the Boston ladies;
A little of last years blue blood dreams and screams in the ditch.
Comforted, I press on—and on—perfectly happy.

4.

Whether or not we *are* heading toward Boston
(And even the question of whether I'm *perfectly* happy)
I leave to another time—a time full of lakes—and crickets!
Meanwhile I drive past Waltham again, gaining more time,
Somewhere on the road to or away from Boston . . .
Thinking of the Boston ladies I have a powerful erection!
High as the Dakota mountains! High as the great mountain near Fargo!

The Passion of the Heavenly Detective

On the film set's formal garden the curse of all curses
Falls on the famous actors: the awful deed has been done.
(Our hero, in silk pyjamas, is at home cleaning his gun.)
Off stage, like a fallen soul or a trio of horses,

A scream still sounds. Our hero does not stir.
Shaving, holding a mirror to Nature, he pondering points
To the Human Condition. Then, with nard and with oil, anoints
The galvanized decorum of his hair.

Then among the stars the heavenly detective wanders,
Suspect to suspect, resolving to solve—be it ill, be it well—
What he considers the perfect crime. Who the hell
Is guilty? The literary Hawkshaw wonders.

Is it the star, sweet Evelyn Laye from Eden,
Nebraska, who sprang fully formed from the richly umbraed side
Of McAdam, the Pythagorean producer, under whose hide
(Surprise!) the golden and dancing rib was hidden?

The world (that groans in its bed when her fabulous name
Troubles its pragmatic sleep)thinks: Is beauty aught but devil-

Ment? For does it not lead to her ivory gates of evil
From whence proceedeth the sorrows of sin and dream?

Or is the crime perhaps some secret canker
Of the script itself—put in by the crochety alcoholic
Writer? Is the villain the villain, so blond and brachycephalic?
And is the satanic stranger a New York banker?

All are suspect to our hero the Private Eye:
Producer, director, star. A cop with a flashing stick
Patrols the garden. Above, the constellations tick.
(The wagon is waiting to take them all away)—

If he could only think like Micky Spillane!
Our hero thinks; what a simple matter to fill with hot lead
The sinful sinner (though it be in the belly or in the head)
And then with Miss Laye to fall in a sexual swound!

But, dreaming, he is aware of the sudden burning
Look on the face of the clock (it is Human Saving Time)
Great God! is he the gilt fall guy, scapegoat for the crime?
He thought it was only a play! And, warily turning,

He turns his weathercock head and Alas! and Alack!
The mortal drama now can have no happy ending.
He was not born to suffer though he suffer to be borne past mending
As he rides through Gethsemane Fair in his Cadillac.

Envoi

Oh hopeful burgess in the darkened theatre
Waiting for the Salvation Follies to go on—
It is enough that you know that your hero is gone,
That neither today nor tomorrow will you see your main feature.

Too bad that today there is little or the wrong kind of love,
And that neither yourself nor your friends will suffer the pain
Of man's passion. The agon is called on account of rain.
Above the garden the stars, or the signs, wink on, wink off.

Mr. Nobody of Nowhere Picks a Card

The distinguished magician with the whisky hands
Selects a card and any card will do.
Turns it face out, a mirror to the void,
But not the void reflects—oh, image is you!

Gorgeous Jack with a Jill at each elbow
And a glad eye cocked at the giveaway world!
It is promised yours at the flick of the wrist.
But if the magic goes wrong and you are hurled

Into the common hell of uncertainty?
Hell is for others. The fingers crawl
Over jokers and kings, but your lucky card,
Like an ace of nothing, is nowhere at all.

Then the black-hatted sharpie, blowing a tin horn
For the next shift, enters, jingling his charm
(A double double-eagle on his watch chain)
A shotgun, like sweet reason, on his arm,

And commands you to the factory of unfixed forms
Where the millions scuffle without suit or number
For their daily bread or the price of a headstone,
A play from the discard. What cogging sleights encumber

Your knightly card! Then, faceless and obscene,
It finally shows. Ah, were you not born
Lucky? Who stole the cunning of your hand?
What Christ was slain on that unhappy morn?

170

Successions

Whoever drives commands the speed that kills.
Loving cups, loves, sports cars, the heads of bears—
We show the trophies of our varied skills.

The fatal elegance that power distills
Unnerves the hunted, leads them into snares.
Whoever drives desires the speed that kills.

The Cross-cut slaves that stank on Roman hills
Invented godhead's posture unawares:
We show the trophies of our famous skills.

Let man be perfected of his ancient ills!
So say the Doctors and the doctrinaires.
(Whoever drives acquires the speed that kills.)

This dream comes down to purges and to pills:
The capitally sick are hanged in the squares—
We show the trophies of our cherished skills.

Neither papal successions nor Bolshevik wills
Insure old bones against heretic heirs.
Whoever drives deserves the speed that kills.
We show the trophies of our fatal skills.

Yes

We were born here
In the trench of a dead tree
Where the revolutionaries gather
Passing the leaves one to another

171

Two Songs from
"The Hunted Revolutionaries"
for Henry Winston

1.

He imagines the great demons of
the four corners of his country

The violent darkness claims us all:
The indifferent demon of the North
Sends his abstract anguish forth,
Tall as you are and more tall.
The violent darkness claims us all.

Tall as you are and more tall,
The impotent demon of the South
Tears the tongue from the honest mouth.
The violent darkness claims us all,
Tall as you are and more tall.

The violent darkness claims us all:
The mechanical demon of the East—
The inflated demon of the West—
Tall as you are and more tall,
The violent darkness claims us all.

The violent darkness claims us all:
Now all your angels summon forth,
From East and West and South and North,
Tall as you are, and more tall.

2.

He calls upon the powers of earth

The dark is in love with forms of light.
Angel of conscience of the North,
Assure all mortals mortal worth!
Stars shine clearest in darkest night:
I summon the angel of the North.

Stars shine clearest in darkest night.
O randy angel of the South,
Be lust of joy in the fields of sloth!
An indifferent joy is man's secret fate:
I summon the angel of the South.

An indifferent joy is our secret fate.
Anarchic angel of the West,
In solidarity bind what's loosed!
All bitterness in time grows sweet:
I summon the angel of the West.

All bitterness in time grows sweet.
Shepherding angel of the East,
Organize concord in the breast!
The dark is in love with forms of light:
I summon the angel of the East.

The dark is in love with forms of light,
Tall as you are and more tall.
Though the violent darkness claim us all
An indifferent joy is our secret fate.
The stars shine clearest in darkest night.
All bitterness in time grows sweet.

Figures in an Allegorical Landscape: the
Carpenter of the American Concentration Camps

Someone is building the house of my death—
And he knows less about it than I do.
The hammer blows clap with his heart,
And every stroke is money and luck—
White Laplands of potatoes, red Soviets of steak,
A Golden Ind of corn—good eating every day.
I'm eaten alive by this presumptious fellow,
The sleepy caterpillar of a different dream.

    O Elected Landscapes! Deserts of our Hope,
    Slough of Despond, Mountain of Desire—
    This ticking Pulse which builds that gallows Time—
    (And Changeling or Prince or Fairy Godmother)
    —Are these elected too? This Union Carpenter
    of Concentration Camp, this Giant Despair?
    Then what is the meaning of Maine or Medicine Hat?
    And where is the elected landscape of my death?

Always I hear him knocking like a guest,
This Carpenter (who is also the Just Man).
Few roles are chosen: he must choose who can
While Venus burns in the constellation of Hunger.
So—I hear that knocking with more love than anger:
But have no right to forgive him for any other man.
He battens on my death. And over and over
His hammer taps in code: All men are brothers.

Proletarian in Abstract Light

Now on the great stage a silence falls.
In the long shudder toward collapse and birth,
There enters, singing, the muffled shape of a future.
He has no face; his hands are bloody;
He is for himself; he is not to please you.

> *You have stolen my labor*
> *You have stolen my name*
> *You have stolen my mystery*
> *You have stolen the moon*

The coldness of song goes on in his barbarous tongue.
The hours condense like snow. The marble weight
Of his dream, like a heavy cloud, leans on your glass houses.
Expropriated of time, he begins himself in *his* name;
He stamps his null on your day; the future collapses toward him:

> *I do not want your clocks*
> *I do not want your God*
> *I do not want your statues*
> *I do not want your love*

Blues for Cisco Houston

More than nine hundred miles from home now Cisco—
Poor boy, gone underground to the final proletariat,
Old Blue following possum in the new ground corn
In the blaze of your death, by the light of your incendiary guitar.

Vessel of light, that black gut-box you carried!
Transport of insurrectionary calendars between Spain and Cuba

175

Bringing to rebels the hot Word, the machine guns of flowers and
 humming birds
Through the money-talking loaves and fishes of the God-blessed
 corporate sea.

In season the moth wing frosts the lamp with incandescent
Mortality. And beyond the frets and freights, half steps,
Stops, changes of time and times—*this train don't carry no
Rustlers, whores nor tin horn hustlers.* Gone. Glory train. Blazing
 guitar.

But here was a man come with a miracle in his bindle!
Winter multitudes warmed at the electric bread of your song,
The butterfly slept secure at the center of the Bomb,
And the Revolution caught fire wherever you came to town.

Elegy for Hart Crane

The fifth angel blows and a star falls in the bottomless pit.
The armless post card blows along on the wind.
One star comes out to unlock the gate of midnight.
In the drunken ocean the islands are walking in their sleep.

Walking the slack wire between dark and dark
A tree forgets itself, lets fall blue eggs
Which opening let loose Simple Simon
Who turns a machine gun on the chocolate sheep.

And the sixth angel blows and a light of arrows
Feathered with eyes falls from the angry moon.
If help is coming it better be coming soon.
When Euclid dances, Algebra falls at his feet.

You, Yannis Ritsos

A bone harrow to rake the barren infernal salt.

An oar
Struck into the sand
Above tidemark

The Deaths of the Poets
Winter 1972

They went away in the cold, in the time when the nights are long,
Flying in the nearest direction to where all months are south.
Leaving behind their scouting reports from our old war,
They parachute forever toward fields as white and blank as a page.

Route Song and Epitaph

Living on catastrophe, eating the pure light
What have we come to but the mother dark?
Over our heads, obscurely, the stars work
Heedless. They did not invent the night.

Memory of a Prophet

I remember him in the time before the fall of the city;
Before they locked up the moon, or drained the light from the stone.
He was worried by women with green eyes, I remember,
Remembering his excessively prophetic style:

"Sun in Sagittarius! November, smoky with evil,
Poisons our sultry blood!" I smile. But now, in the street,
A licensed thief makes off with the final human conviction.
He wrote "We meet on Thursday after the second Tuesday."

Or maybe Tuesday after the second Thursday. It's long
Since I saw him, but now and again I seem to meet him in dreams,
Or out of the river (beside still waters) my following ghost,
My weird, looks up at me. And once, while shaving—

"Knives are deadly for you! Cover your trail!" Too late.
That odd disease of time makes real all prophecy.
The blood on the midnight street, the hunted, the jailed, the exiled
Cry down the dark that seems to have no end.

And, in *that* dark, Mister Average C. Citizen
Passes, his hand absentmindedly stuck in the maw
Of a voting machine. He can't get loose. He's stoned
At the Arkansas bottom of the national nightmare.

So it goes. Gunfire at midnight. The police arrive for the looting.
Now that I think of it, his style seems hardly excessive.
In the time of ignitible cities the words sound plainer;
And in those days even the poets thought it enough to warn:

"*These rooks in rainy wind. Crows cry. November
A hooded evil!*" Ten years ago he wrote it!
Prophetic. "Meeting at five past forever, see. Remember:
Wait. And sign no papers—wait for me—see no one."

178

Again: This Room, in This Street, in This Time

Who runs may read—and now's the time for running.
Was it—yes—Sy Devant who left all those notes behind
Bunged in a bottle (the script as clean as a whistle
And the blood all dry) that the ebb tide dropped on my desk.

Tomorrow's news always arrives today:
"An alien land"—but then all lands are alien.
"Natives unfriendly. Our first patrols were ambushed."
He writes with the explorer's usual dramatic unction.

A far country, that one, where the horses don't have shadows
And the moon sings like a bone.
                                Along about noontime
The notes drop on my desk "Smoke on the mountains,
The roads washed out by rain." Next day: "Mutiny."

So, day unto day, and the notes arriving
Each one more desperate and more familiar.
"We came through the passes, we crossed the black mountain in snow."
When did it happen? In what far land was that?

Little by little the geography settles and fixes:
"A place between three rivers." "A city shaped like a crescent."
"Many in jails and the poets all turned cowards
So that they have no honor in this country.

"Now we have a wide road to the west,
And beyond the mountains the sea and a smoky city.
Ambushed again last night." Finally:
"The cities stinking of commerce and the whole interior savage."

Little by little the landscape grows fixed and familiar.
I wait for the last installment, which now at my desk
Lousy, bearded, in rags, my twin and stranger
Writes while a siren prowls like a wolf on the street.

179

The Last War Poem of the War
for Jimmy McGrath

Now is the first day of autumn, all politics and pose:
The generals talk war in parable, the poets in prose,
The living walk round in circles, the upright dead lie in rows.

Half upright in a chair in the body in which I die,
But not contained in the prolonged circle of your day,
How easy to write poems of your Other Way!

How easy to proclaim your perfect sacrifice:
Pro patria mori, the Hanged God dies;
The orators walk widdershins across your eyes.

And easy enough for me, with my questionable needs,
To enhymn you in the fencing of my personal creeds
Or feel you've gone wilder than the blown autumn seeds.

All easy variants of the need to forget—
To shove you under for good: and in any case what net
Could take you now? But I will solve you yet,

Though nineteenth century poets in contemporary poses
(Or generals) rime our bad blood into grass and roses.
Or wash it out of their paper towers with hoses.

Reading the Names of the Vietnam War Dead

For a long day and a night we read the names:
Many thousand brothers fallen in the green and distant land . . .

Sun going south after the autumn equinox.
By night the vast moon: "Moon of the Falling Leaves";

Our voices hoarse in the cold of the first October rains.
And the long winds of the season to carry our words away.

The citizens go on about their business.
By night sleepers condense in the houses grown cloudy with
    dreams.
By day a few come to hear us and leave, shaking their
    heads
Or cursing. On Sunday the moral animal prays in his church.

It is Fall; but a host of dark birds flies toward the cold
    North.
Thousands of dense black stones fall forever through the
    darkness under the earth.

Long Distance from a War

A child and a girl—my wife—emptied my house
In a forced march toward the firefly in his blazing village.
There, in the uncharred rosebush
The insects are enacting a bloodless Gettysburg—
The centipede and millipede centuries
Before bells rang or cows belled or bellbuoys and
               telephones clanged in anger.

In the moment my poem swam in from the sea and stars
(Over the cows exploding in Viet Nam fields)
Edison extended his claim and accident.
Television opened a poisoned eye in my head.
My eyelids rang up like murderous flags
Behind which all my love had been going on.

Something Is Dying Here

In a hundred places in North Dakota
Tame locomotives are sleeping
Inside the barricades of bourgeois flowers:
Zinnias, petunias, johnny-jump-ups—
Their once wild fur warming the public squares.

Something is dying here.
                   And perhaps I, too—
My brain already full of the cloudy lignite of eternity . . .

I invoke an image of my strength.
                        Nothing will come.
Oh—a homing lion perhaps
                   made entirely of tame bees;
Or the chalice of an old storage battery, loaded
With the rancid electricity of the nineteen thirties
Cloud harps iconographic blood
Rusting in the burnt church of my flesh . . .

But nothing goes forward:
The locomotive never strays out of the flower corral
The mustang is inventing barbwire the bulls
Have put rings in their noses . . .

The dead here
Will leave behind a ring of autobodies,
Weather-eaten bones of cars where the stand-off failed—

    Strangers: go tell among the Companions:
    These dead weren't put down by Cheyennes or Red Chinese:
    The poison of their own sweet country has brought them here.

The Rituals at the Chapel Perilous
for the black revolutionaries,
Henry Winston & Angela Davis

We heard the cries, the fighting in the streets,
At the Continuous Political Meeting of the Present.
Someone was dying on every corner
As we went in, but an impersonal music
Covered his cries with art. At the tables
The speaking had started. A professional mourner
Began a traditional lament for the Good,
And the waiters danced in with the abstract food.

Then the limber artillery of the orators
Was trained on that butterfly of speculation
The Historic Moment: which exists, for rhetoric,
Forever, like the flower in the heart of the lotus.
And then was strict reality unlaced
By light-fingered orgsecs of the metaphoric
Who can-canned precisely a ritual of belief,
One last cliché, a rose between their teeth.

And, with the thunder of this entertainment,
The cries of the suffering were lost on the malignant
Dark. The tailor-tongued speakers wrapped the dying
In shrouds of formulae. The blood that streamed
In the firmament turned to a flotation process,
And one statistic tear wept all the grief of crying.
O mathematic priests! You once understood
All pain consubstantial with the body and blood.

Word lost, world lost. Dead ceremony left
The hall a calculus of wish: the light
Went green as undersea, where, ghostly fish,
We swam through objects like equations;

183

All pain went formal as the ritual failed
Of resurrection — like a broken dish
The Grail was borne away. Then cock-crow! Christ!
Your black and magic light restored our eyes————

A transudation of reality
Stains the ghost world like a veronica:
All colors in your name. The anonymous host,
Weeping at midnight in the stony streets,
Changes from number to identity
In your mouth. And all that empty New World coast
Of Hope condenses lovers like a dew.
Thus, with your grace, the world begins anew.

Forgive the tedium of my argument
And simple idiom. I praise, because, with you,
The crying became human again, and lathes
Remembered to turn, birds to sing, and language
Its meaning. It is because of you
A mortal glory in the inhuman hour
Has been restored. We too, now, bring to play
The popular magic of our common day.

O'Leary's Last Wish:
In Case the Revolution Should Fail

I want to be buried in Arlington Cemetery,
Somewhere at the patriotic center of the American Death,
With my bones full of the sleepy dynamite of the class struggle
And the time-bomb of the century under my private's shirt.

I want to lie there and tick like a pulse among the defunct
Heroes, the quiet deserters of their own body and blood—
The ones who stood on expensive roads in the total shell fire of money
Being cut off at the balls for their own and the public good.

184

I'll be there, the anti-bourgeois neutrino of the irreconciliable
                              proletariat,
Among the tame terrene charges of those patriotic stiffs.
Contra-Destiny Factors ring midnight, but there's no gold in their
                              veins;
Cock crow chimes thrice. Reveille. No one is stirring yet

But under the ghost-overgrown honortabs to the wars,
The real estate and spirit-money my fellow-death-workers have won,
Is the Word of the Four Last Things of the Working Class, the rumored
Revolution of the Dead which Heaven, and the Boss, want put down.

Nevertheless, I'm still here, Hell's partisan, with my anti-god bomb,
Agitating toward the day when these stony dead
Shall storm up out of the ground in their chalky battalions
To judge wars, Presidents, Fates, God and His Own Elect.

Political Song for the Year's End

1.

The darkness of the year begins,
In which we hunt the summer kings.
(Who will kill Cock Robin when
His breast is cheery with his sin?)
And when, transfigured in the skies,
The starry, hunted hero dies,
The redemptive rain of his golden blood
Quickens the barley of the Good.
Sing to the moon, for every change must come.

2.

The democratic senator
's conjunctive to the warrior star,

185

And Market wavers into trine
As the geared heavens tick and shine.
The Worker snores; the Poet drowses
Through all his literary Houses;
The Goose hangs high, the Wife lays low,
And all the children are on Snow.
Sing to the moon, for every change is known.

3.

Each role must change. Each change must come.
Turning, we make the great Wheel turn
In a rage of impotence, forth and back
Through the stations of history's zodiac.
Caught in the trap of our daily bread,
A hopeful, stumbling multitude,
We surrender and struggle, save and slay,
Turning the Wheel in the ancient way.
Sing to the moon; for every change must pass.

4.

And now with an indifferent eye
We see our savior hunted by,
Into that furious dark of time
His only death may all redeem.
And when at last that time is grown
When all the great shall be cast down,
We rejoice to praise who now is slain—
For the darkness of the year is come.
Sing to the moon, for every change is known.

Gone Away Blues

Sirs, when you are in your last extremity,
When your admirals are drowning in the grass-green sea,
When your generals are preparing the total catastrophe—
I just want you to know how you can not count on me.

> I have ridden to hounds through my ancestral halls,
> I have picked the eternal crocus on the ultimate hill,
> I have fallen through the window of the highest room,
> But don't ask me to help you 'cause I never will.

Sirs, when you move that map-pin how many souls must dance?
I don't think all those soldiers have died by happenstance.
The inscrutable look on your scrutable face I can read at a glance—
And I'm cutting out of here at the first chance.

> I have been wounded climbing the second stair,
> I have crossed the ocean in the hull of a live wire,
> I have eaten the asphodel of the dark side of the moon,
> But you can call me all day and I just won't hear.

O patriotic mister with your big ear to the ground,
Sweet old curly scientist wiring the birds for sound,
O lady with the Steuben glass heart and your heels so rich and round—
I'll send you a picture postcard from somewhere I can't be found.

> I have discovered the grammar of the Public Good,
> I have invented a language that can be understood,
> I have found the map of where the body is hid,
> And I won't be caught dead in your neighborhood.

O hygienic inventer of the bomb that's so clean,
O lily white Senator from East Turnip Green,
O celestial mechanic of the money machine—
I'm going someplace where nobody makes your scene.

Good-by, good-by, good-by,
Adios, au 'voir, so long,
Sayonara, dosvedanya, ciao,
By-by, by-by, by-by.

Thomas McGrath teaches in the English Department at Moorhead State College in Minnesota.